TO:
Talla—

WISHING YOU CONTINUED
SUCCESS AND ALL THE
BEST!!

KEEP BEING A BADASS!!

George
Custer

SECRETS TO BECOMING
A FINANCIAL BADASS

www.mascotbooks.com

Secrets to Becoming a Financial Badass

For more information, please contact:
Mascot Books
620 Herndon Parkway #320
Herndon, VA 20170
info@mascotbooks.com

CPSIA Code: PBANG0518A
Library of Congress Control Number: 2018903409
ISBN-13: 978-1-68401-134-6

Printed in the United States

SECRETS TO BECOMING A
FINANCIAL GENIUS

BADASS

George Kroustalis

TO ALL THE FUTURE
FINANCIAL BADASSES
OUT THERE WHO KNOW
YOU DON'T NEED TO
BE RICH, BUT YOU
MIGHT AS WELL BE.

TABLE OF CONTENTS

PROLOGUE

"**G**ood morning, my name is George Kroustalis and I'm with [fill in the blank], how's everybody feeling this morning?"

• • •

"Ah, c'mon, you can do better than that! How's everybody *doing* this morning!?"

That's how I start them...nearly every one of them. The 401(k) enrollment meetings. My 20 minutes to act like I'm that guy who knows all and to preach to the newbies that yes, there is a way to retire—and this is how you do it, step by step. Some are long-time employees who either want to get out of work for half an hour, or who love watching me present. (I'd love to think it's the latter, but who are we kidding?) But mostly it's the newbies, the new hires. Yes, new participants who, for the most part, have never been exposed to a retirement plan. For many, it may be their first job, so they don't even know what it is!

That's where I come in—the financial advisor. I'm here for them; not only to educate them on all they need to know about their company's greatest benefit ever (the 401(k) plan), but to show them how easy it is to join, and where they should invest their money. I come in every enrollment period. It's really not that complicated, especially once you show them what I call the "magic mountain chart."

If you haven't seen it, trust me, you will soon enough. The one that starts with so little money ($1k or $10k) and after years and years of something called compounding, *voilà*, the line has gone from bottom left straight up to the right corner, and your $1k is worth a hundred times more. (I told you it was magic.)

That's what I'd done for much of my early career. And the meetings usually end the same way, sometimes with a standing ovation...but usually just a sitting one. For the most part, I enjoy it. Actually, I love it. The best part is towards the end of the meeting, when I put all the pieces together (from tax advantages to the benefits), and I show them that mountain chart. I look around the room from face to face, yearning for eye contact, and then, I find it; that gleam in someone's eyes as they nod and ask me before I can even finish, "How do I sign up?" Anyone in this room can easily do it, and they get it...it feels awesome!

But it was this one particular meeting, after the typical Q & A, that ended a little differently...

"George," I heard a voice behind me say, as I was walking back to my car.

I turned around. "Yes, how are you?" I greeted him...

INTRODUCTION

I'm doing fine," he replied. "Listen, you probably don't remember me, but I sat in on one of your presentations about twelve years ago. At the time, I didn't believe much of what you said, about how saving a few hundred a month could mean having tens of thousands down the road. But I joined the plan that day, just to see what would happen, and today I have more money in my account than I ever thought I would have in my life! So...I just wanted to say 'thank you.'"

That's how this story begins, one Friday afternoon in October.

Wow! WTF just happened? I thought. I wasn't sure what to say, so I just said a "thank you." He smiled and just wandered off, and I was left standing alone, never having expected that the day would take such a wild turn.

My interaction that afternoon was the **spark that lit the fire** for this project, and the *reason* I wrote it was to simplify the message so that **anyone** can learn these basics and take charge of their financial futures while enjoying the ride along the way.

I got in my car and started my journey home, but I couldn't get it out of my head. I began revisiting some of the presentations I had given before, and I was pumped that the message I had been trying to get across had not only been successfully received, but had manifested itself in such a visible way. Of course, that was the goal, right? To encourage people to take command of their futures by saving and investing wisely and to take advantage of what their employers had to offer? I never thought I would see the impact firsthand.

As time went on, and a drink or two into the evening, ideas kept popping into my head that I couldn't shake. If I could affect one person like this, why not more? How could I get this message across to more people? *Especially* young people just starting out. I wanted to teach people who weren't already secure in a career. I wanted to help people who were just starting off their working lives, or who were still in school; people I might not ever meet, but who all could benefit from these ideas, including those who may not even have a career or full-time job. White collar, blue collar, any-color collar you like—it didn't matter. **Everyone young, in the end, has one thing in common: when it comes to retirement planning (i.e., having a shitload of money later in life) and investing, time is on their side. Period. End of story.**

After all, despite how complex and boring financial planning can be, the message really is a simple one at its core: start saving early, and let time and the power of compounding (we'll get there too!) do the work. I still wonder, how could something so simple seem so difficult, or obscure, to most people? Why didn't they teach us this in school?

So I began a list of ways to get this message out. I considered YouTube videos and street performance (The Amazing Juggling Advisor just wasn't meant to be), but ultimately settled on what you have in front of you: this book—a simple, easy-to-read one that would be of use for people at all stages of their educational, vocational, and professional lives.

I had never written a book before and quickly got excited about the challenge. Of course, I knew early on that it wouldn't be easy, since finance isn't the most exciting material. It can be very dry stuff, and I'm sure a few of you have probably already rolled your eyes at the thought of a guy getting excited for a PowerPoint presentation!

No, no, no, I wanted this to be *on point*. I wanted it to be relevant— not just about saving early and investing, because duh, that's easy. I wanted it to be about owning your shit. That's right: being large and in charge. If you can handle your finances early on in your career and life, whatever you want to call it…from graduating high school into your first real job…you are more than halfway there, on the road. You are *golden*.

"Why?" you might ask. Because that's the time in your life when you can do some really dumb things, financially—things that are hard to recover from. It could take years, or decades. But more importantly—on the flipside—it is also a time when you can do a few really smart things that will set you up for life. This book is gonna teach you about that: both the dumb things and how to avoid them, and the smart things and how to do them.

But you can't become a financial badass by just learning about building a comfortable retirement or nest egg. You gotta get to retirement first! There are a lot of years between now and then—between now and when you get to stop working. So let's learn how to get to then, while still living the good life.

The more I thought about the idea, the more I heard a voice (this may or may not have been Shia) telling me to *just do it*. But we have to do it differently. Differently than those long, monotonous novels that go on and on about saving and investing and blah, blah, blah. I began thinking about what turned me off about finance books. Most of them are too long, so I decided to keep this short—under 150 pages. Let's be honest, who actually likes books that are *too* long, especially ones with pages of equations?

Well, here goes nothing! What you have in front of you is the first of its kind. A short, easy read, in three sections, on the essentials of what can be done with our money.

- **Save it!** (okay, not so fun!)
- **Spend it!** (the fun stuff)
- **Invest it!** (all of the above...and more!)

WE DON'T NEED NO EDUCATION (BUT SERIOUSLY, WE DO!)

When I first began my research, I came across something that frankly shocked me. I had gotten to thinking about why I hadn't learned hardly any of this material when I was younger. It hadn't been taught in my school...but surely this sort of stuff was being taught in other schools, right?

Well, it turns out that very few states require that their public school systems have financial literacy classes as a required part of the curriculum. In fact, as of this writing, fewer than half of states require that students take some kind of economic course, and only *five* require a standalone course on personal finance (the topic of this book). The ideas you will be exposed to in this book are very important; I would say even necessary. Let's face it, basic money skills are essential for everyday life, and yet only a handful of states require their students learn them.

So a main focus of this book you have in front of you is education. Yes, we know so little! ***Just think if seniors in high school were taught the value of money at 17 or 18,*** instead of having to wait until much later in life and find out the hard way...

It doesn't have to be this way, where so many young people know so little. By reading this book, you will gain a roadmap, a guide to not only learning *about* saving, debt, credit scores, student loans, and the scary, unknowable mystery, aka the stock market; you are going to learn the *how* and *why* of saving, spending, and investing. It doesn't matter where you are from or what school you went to; you will learn more than enough to make you a badass!

So we have settled on some goals. We want to retire comfortably, we want to make smart moves early, we want to educate ourselves, and we want to enjoy life to the fullest in the meantime. This book will give you the tools to have your cake and eat it too—maybe not at the same time, 'cause that could be illegal, but more often than not. Cheers!

CHAPTER ONE: SAVE!

We're going to begin with a simple rule. As a matter of fact, it's so simple a concept, you might wonder how I could write an entire chapter about saving! Our simple rule is: just because you have money, doesn't mean you should spend it!

This might seem counterintuitive, because after all, what is money for if not spending? Money just sitting in a bank account or hiding in a sock drawer (don't do this) isn't doing anything; you could say its purpose isn't being realized. The key skill we want to learn here is knowing when to spend money, and when to just leave it in the sock drawer (but seriously, don't do this).

Let's imagine two friends, Jack and Jen. They are juniors in high school, and both have a job during the summer at Jack's uncle's green bean packaging plant, making sure labels aren't put on the cans upside down. This might not sound glamorous, but give them a break; it's their first real job and they could use the money!

Every Friday, Jack and Jen get a check for their hard work making sure the world's green bean cans are legible. Jack goes to the bank that issued the check and gets his precious $134.76. From there, he goes right to Bert's Gas and Chow (which sells pretty much what you would expect) and gets some junk food. Usually he meets up with friends a little later, sees a movie, gets some dinner...you can see where this is going. By the end of the weekend, he has exhausted his earnings. But this is okay, right? After all, he lives with his parents, eats most of his meals with them for free, and doesn't have a car or anything else that would cut into his fun money. He doesn't *need* to do anything with the money, so why not spend it? That's what it's for!

Jen, on the other hand, goes to the same bank and deposits her check. She takes some cash out to see a movie and grab a bite to eat with friends that Friday night, but leaves most of it at the bank in something called a "savings account." She has bigger plans for her growing green bean fortune. By the end of the summer, her goal is realized: she has enough money for the down payment on a used, yet reliable, classic 1969 white Mustang. You can imagine Jack's surprise when she drives up to school the first day of their senior year, Lana Del Rey's "Ride" blasting from the speakers.

The point here isn't necessarily to say that Jen made the right decision (or that she has great taste in music), but to demonstrate how spending money just because it is immediately available isn't always the right and most rewarding decision. Jack and Jen might not have to pay rent or medical bills, but that doesn't mean that their cash on hand is freely available.

Let's talk about the ins and outs of saving. This is going to be a very different practice depending on a lot of factors, but let's stick with Jack and Jen for the time being.

There are two main options for our heroes: checking and savings accounts. Checking accounts simply hold money (with a few restrictions based on the bank) and come with an ATM/debit card that will let you spend it. Savings accounts tend to have more restrictions, but the account holder earns interest over time based on the account balance.

Now, way back in the day, savings accounts were much more rewarding than they are now. It wasn't uncommon for an account holder to earn quite a bit simply by leaving money in his or her account. For example, in the late 1980s and early 1990s, it was possible to set up a savings account with interest rates in the 9 to 11 percent range. Let's do some math and see what this would look like for our protagonists.

Jack and Jen make $134.76 a week, or $539.04 a month. If that all went into a savings account with an initial balance of $1.00 and an interest rate of 10 percent compounded monthly, then at the end of a year, the account balance would be $6,774.45. Just depositing the money into an account with *no* interest earned would net $6,468.48. This means that just by letting all their money sit in the savings account without withdrawing any earns them $305.97! Free money!

Sadly, these levels of interest in savings accounts are a thing in the past. These days, Jack and Jen would be lucky to find a savings account that offered more than 1.5 percent interest. There is a long, complicated story behind this drastic drop in interest rates, and if you want to learn more, see the sources at the end of this book. The long and the short of it is: savings accounts just aren't worth the restrictions unless you have a relatively large balance, are making relatively large, consistent deposits, or intend to use one as an emergency fund or for long term savings (more on this later).

GET AHEAD OF SAVING

Many people make the mistake of thinking that only *extra* money should be saved. First, they set aside money for groceries, then they set aside money for travel expenses, then they set aside money for rent or a mortgage, then for utilities and supplies for Ted's birthday party and a new faucet because the old one is leaking and on and on. Well, the end of the month rolls around and these people have no *extra* money left. It's all been spent.

Budgeting can be boring, but it is important, so we are going to touch on it in this section and even look at different approaches to it. Spending money without thinking about it, and avoiding planning for the future, will usually end badly. If you don't take a proactive approach to budgeting, you might end up broke and dying under a bridge. All right, that might be an over-exaggeration, but you get the picture! The point is: pay attention to your budget, and have a game plan for spending and saving your money. Even if you aren't the budgeting type (I know I never was!) you can get to the core pretty simply: *save first, spend afterwards!*

However, and this is a big one, it is possible to *over-budget*. This means you spend so much time planning ahead, chopping up your earnings, and earmarking certain funds for certain things that you end up working against yourself. You end up having spent all your money, with nothing left over to save. Let's be honest, there are very few people in a position where they can spend their monthly income in ways that seem appropriate, then have extra money just lying around, begging to be thrown into a high-interest savings account. I know I'm not one of those people, and if you really want to get rich, we should assume you aren't either.

This phenomenon happens because we sometimes have a hard time perceiving the difference between a "want" and a "need." Sometimes that leaky faucet doesn't need replacing. It sure would be nice to have a clean, shiny one that works, but maybe see if you can fix it yourself! Ted is a great guy and all, but do you really need to rent a margarita maker for his birthday party? These types of decisions, which might seem so little when they come up, slowly accumulate and really eat into our finances. There is a solution, however, that can easily keep this slow death of our bank accounts from happening.

That solution is so important, I will give it to you this way:

SAVE MONEY BEFORE YOU SPEND MONEY.

What do I mean by this? It is very simple. When you get paid, don't immediately start paying bills. Don't go to the grocery store. And whatever you do, don't even think about that buying that new avatar skin for your game. The first thing you should do is set aside money for the future. We can get wrapped up in the details later, but whatever the amount that you settle on to set aside from your monthly income, be it 10 percent or $500, be sure that the first thing you do is put it somewhere you can't spend it. Another way to think about it is that you are simply paying yourself first. If you have to, think about your future fund as a bill...you've GOT to pay it! So,

PAY YOURSELF FIRST!

Make Saving Make Sense

So, we know we have to save money and budget appropriately. We know we want to pay ourselves first. But how? How do we get organized and manage our money in an ordered, useful way? The first step towards successful saving is understanding what our costs are.

By costs, I mean the ugly stuff. The stuff we all have to do but hate doing. You know what I mean:

- Rent
- Utilities
- Car Payments
- Car Insurance
- Cell Phone
- Food (okay, food is great, you got me there!)
- Debt Payments (if any)

And so on and so forth. These sorts of costs we are going to call essential costs. These are things that we *have* to pay in order to stay alive, healthy, and lawsuit-free.

Next we have investments. There is a lot of variety here, and we will have a more in-depth look at them later in this book. For now, just think of them as costs that are going to help you down the road.

There are many things that we might not need in order to survive, but are still very reasonable purchases. Things like buying a house or getting married or getting a slightly less beat-up car. These aren't things that we can just purchase off a single paycheck, so we need to save for them.

Not only is it smart to have an emergency fund, you *need* one. They are non-negotiable. The world is an unpredictable place, and you should do the best you can to prepare for things like car repairs, paying an insurance deductible for medical costs, and things like that.

And finally, in order to remain sane, we all need to treat ourselves on occasion. No one wants to eat rice and beans every night for dinner, even if it does save a ton of money. Screw that! So consider movie tickets, eating out, and other things like that to be extra.

So, in very broad strokes, we have:

- Essential Costs
- Short-term Saving
- Long-term Saving and Investing

- Emergency Funds
- Treat Yourself

Your monthly paychecks are going to be divided between these five broad categories. The next step is going to be deciding how to split your income between these categories so that you can effectively manage your money. Begin by making a list of the essential costs and their amounts. Here is an example of what that might look like on a per-month basis:

RENT	$950
UTILITIES (GAS, ELECTRIC, INTERNET)	$250
CAR PAYMENT	$175
CAR INSURANCE	$115
CELL PHONE	$85
CREDIT CARD PAYMENT	$65
FOOD	$300
TOTAL (ESSENTIAL COSTS)	$1,940

If you are making $40,000 a year, your take-home pay after taxes will be around $2,500 a month. This leaves us with $560 a month to divvy up into those other four categories. We won't deal with investments in any depth here, since that will be a big focus of later parts of this book. Trust me, we are saving the best for last! There is also some complication, since contributions to 401(k) plans occur pre-tax, which means that money never actually hits your checking account. For the time being, we are going to go with a generally accepted amount to contribute: 6 percent, or $150. Later in this book you will find out more about contributions, yearly limits, recommended contribution percentages, and more. This leaves us with $410. Crazy how quickly it starts to run out! So, we are down to three categories: long-term savings, emergency funds, and treat yourself.

Short-term savings is one of the trickier categories, since it is so goal-driven. Saving for the down payment on a house can be a huge task for some, while others might not be at all interested in buying a house. The same goes with marriage, having children, and so on. Since everyone is going to have different savings goals, I can't really tell you how much to set aside every month based on your unique situation. I can show you *how* to plan, though!

First, lay out your savings priorities. If you want to buy a house, do some research on the real estate in the area you are considering. Zillow and other online services have a wealth of information—particularly historic prices for houses in the area. You can find out from there, and by contacting local real estate agents, what your target should be for a down payment. There are also handy down payment calculators on the web. Once you have a number (for most people, this will be somewhere between $15,000 and $50,000), you have a goal, and the rest is simple math. Decide when you want to be able to make the down payment, and plan accordingly.

Let's say the down payment amount is $15,000. Make up a chart that will give you a concrete idea of when this is doable:

MONTHLY CONTRIBUTION	NUMBER OF MONTHS TO GOAL
$350	43
$250	60
$200	75

If you see yourself staying in a certain area for a while, have a very stable job (hopefully with a retirement plan!), and feel comfortable going without spending in other areas of your life, an aggressive approach like in the first row might be best. If you aren't sure about when you want to buy a house but still want to someday, perhaps setting a small amount into a separate account might be best.

An emergency fund, on the other hand, isn't negotiable. Nothing is worse than being completely unprepared for when shit hits the fan. I can't stress enough the importance of saving money in case something happens, whether it is unexpected car repairs, healthcare costs, or paying for the aftermath of that bachelor party in Vegas that took a turn for the crazy. A common rule of thumb is that your emergency fund target should be the equivalent of your expenses for three to six months. If you lose your job, this is the average amount of time it takes to find a new one. And if you don't lose your job, you will have saved a very decent sum for other types of contingencies. For our hypothetical person making $40,000 a year, the recommended emergency savings would be somewhere between $12,000 and $16,000. This is what is needed to live for those three to six months of job hunting.

How do we translate this figure into monthly savings contributions for an emergency fund? In an ideal world, you should be saving around 10 to 15 percent of your monthly income. In our example, that would be $500. Unfortunately, we are down to $60 to $210, depending on how much we have allocated for long-term savings. So, we turn to a second general rule: the ratio of optional expenses (treat yourself) to savings contributions should be 2 to 3. This means that for every $2 that you have allocated for fun stuff, you save $3. Let's apply this rule and look at the overall monthly finances for our hypothetical hero, assuming he or she wants to set aside a middle-of-the-road amount for a down payment on a house:

RENT	$1,000
UTILITIES	$200
CAR PAYMENT	$175
CAR INSURANCE	$115
CELL PHONE	$85
CREDIT CARD PAYMENT	$65
FOOD	$300
RETIREMENT CONTRIBUTION	$150
LONG-TERM SAVINGS	$150
EMERGENCY SAVINGS	$96
TREAT YOURSELF	$164
TOTAL	$2,500

It goes without saying that these numbers will be drastically different for different people. I know, I know, $164 a month for treating yourself isn't much, highly dependent on what your drink of choice is! Macallan 18 Year might be one hell of a good scotch, but you will eat through your $164 with a few glasses. Some of you might have student loans, some of you might have avoided credit card debt, some of you might have travel expenses comped by employers—the variety is endless.

Like most things, you might need to sacrifice one thing to get more of something else. One size doesn't fit all when it comes to budgets. For example, you might decide to drive a lesser car and reduce your long-term savings so that you can treat yourself with a few extra hundred bucks each month. The important thing is this: **never reduce your contribution to emergency savings**. Roughly one in three Americans don't have enough money to cover a $2,000 emergency expense in the next month. A badass would never let this happen to them! Hopefully this little exercise has given you some guidance on how to approach spreading out your monthly income in a way that addresses all of the important things.

COUNT BY TENS

We are going to revisit these numbers, but first we'll take a look at a budgeting system that a friend of mine told me about years ago. He has gotten by just by doing this, and it is the way to go if you just hate charts and spreadsheets. It is very easy to remember: 10 percent, 20 percent, 30 percent, 40 percent. Let's take $100. Under this system, an optimal way to budget is to pay yourself first $10 (this goes into your investments and retirement funds), dedicate $20 to your home situation (rent or mortgage payment), chalk up $30 to taxes (unfortunately we have no choice in the matter), and then the remaining $40 can be spent how you want. As we have discussed, paying yourself first is one of the *most* important things you can do with your money when you have time and means in your twenties. So, let's take a look at the $2,500 monthly income budget above. Taxed at 30 percent, the actual monthly income would be $3,750. 10 percent [retirement] of that is $375, and 20 percent [housing] is $750. The remaining $1,375 can then be spent on whatever you like, although I recommend you buy clothes, food, and water. You know, the necessities. This system tells us that $950 for housing is a bit too much, and that to keep on track a cheaper place to live should be found. The extra $250 saved from this should be split between retirement investing and other costs. We will use this 10 to 40 percent idea later in the book as a way to demonstrate that you can go virtually anywhere, and do almost anything, while maintaining a careful, responsible personal budget that will help you become truly badass!

SO HOW DO I DO IT?

You get home from a long day at work. On your lunch break, you read this chapter on how to use your money in a constructive way. You spend some time going through the mail to find your utilities bills, your credit card statement, and figure out how much food you need each week. You have put all the data into Excel or on paper, and you are ready to take action. What is the easiest, most stress-free way to get your money to where it needs to be? Thankfully, in this day and age, you have more options than you can possibly use.

This entire process can be automated. You can do some initial set-up, then sit back and let the technological marvels of the day do the dirty work for you. This will spare you the anxiety of having to chop up your paychecks by hand and will minimize the chance that you make a mistake and overspend on one thing at the expense of another. The first of these tools is direct deposit.

When you start a job, you will be given the option of starting direct deposit. Employers love direct deposit, since it saves them the hassle of dealing with paper paychecks. It also is good for the environment, since those pay stubs don't go in the trash. You will need two numbers to fill out the information on the direct deposit form: your bank account number and the routing number. These can be found on the checks for your checking account, a few of which are usually provided for free when you start the account. Of course, we do live in a digital age...so you can also find this information in the online account you will be able to start for your bank account. There are usually two numbers at the bottom of your checks. The first number contains the routing number; this is always a 9-digit number. The second is the bank account number. They both might be preceded by some zeros, depending on the bank; just ignore these.

In about two weeks your paycheck will be automatically deposited into your checking account. Step one complete, but there's more!

There will be an option on your direct deposit form to split up your paycheck between multiple accounts. We can definitely make use of this, because we want the money going towards short-term savings and the emergency fund to gain interest. We have talked about how little interest is earned in savings accounts these days...but something is better than nothing!

I recommend having three accounts to start with and dividing your paycheck between them. The first account will be the checking account; this is the account the bulk of your paycheck will go towards. It will be used for paying bills, buying food, and things like that. The second account will be a savings account and will be where your long-term savings will go (in the example above, this will be $250). The third account will also be a savings account, and will be for the emergency fund ($96 a month in our example). Once you have this set up, you can relax—you are saving for a house and preparing for a rainy day, and you don't have to lift a finger anymore!

Now, on to the checking account. The costs associated with this money can also be automated. Every cell phone company lets you make automated payments; the same is true for the most part when it comes to utilities, car insurance payments, and so on. You can set up most of these payments online and will have some flexibility when it comes to the date of the payment. To do this the smart way, set your automatic payments for the first business day after you get your first paycheck of the month. This way everything is taken care of in a timely fashion, and you don't have to worry about whether funds will be available for other costs later in the month.

When all is said and done, you will be in a situation where all you have to do is go to work and buy groceries. Everything else is done for you. You are essentially saving money for a house, saving money for retirement, and saving money for emergencies passively. At the gym exercising? You're saving. Sleeping? You're a few dollars closer to a comfortable retirement. Driving to work? You're making money that will help you buy a house or get married. Once the day-to-day maintenance of your money is managed automatically, you will begin to see the rewards of carefully planning out your financial activity. Like being able to afford that rocket-powered Jeep you have always wanted.

Saving is a necessary part of many big purchases (a house, a car, diamond-encrusted sneakers, etc.), and there is no way to prepare for certain financial realities without saving. It helps keep you disciplined and earns a bit of interest, which means someone who saves has more future spending potential than someone who burns through their paychecks as soon as they get them. Saving gives you the *freedom* to do more with your money because, well, you have more of it! This is why I like to call saved money your *freedom fund.* Disciplined savers have more money and flexibility, which means there are fewer restrictions on how they spend. I've got to be free...

BANKS EVERYWHERE!

Now let's cover what to look for in a savings account. As mentioned earlier, they usually come with some restrictions when it comes to withdrawals and minimum balances. Here are some things to keep in mind when starting a savings account:

- **Minimum balance requirement.** This one is going to be tough to avoid, but keep shopping around for an account that doesn't have a high requirement. Don't even look twice at a bank that has a $200+ minimum balance requirement. If you need to use your emergency fund, you don't want to have to pay penalties if you drain the account all the way. Smaller banks and credit unions tend to offer very low minimum balance requirements in order to attract more customers; start your search with local credit unions.

- **Monthly fees.** Bigger banks are the main culprit here as well. Avoid savings accounts that charge $5 or more a month just to keep the account open. If you are willing to go with an online-only savings account, you might find some that have *no* monthly fee at all. American Express and Bancorp are two banks that have essentially free online savings accounts. The downside is that they have much lower interest rates.

- **Interest rates.** These days, every bank is stingy when it comes to interest. You're probably not going to find a savings account that offers much more than 1 to 2 percent. And the higher the rate, the more fees are attached to the account. You will need to find an account with the right balance. If you are able to put a lot of money into a savings account each month, you might want to go with an account that has a higher rate, since you won't feel the fees as much and will be able to take advantage of higher earning power. If you can only put a small amount in, high fees will outweigh the benefit of having higher interest so you should go with a cheap or free account.

- **Overdraft fees,** AKA the bane of young people and students everywhere. These things will eat you alive. If you are close to payday and make a few purchases with your debit card and bring your account into the negative, you can expect to pay a crapload in fees. Like, $30 per transaction. You don't want to end up paying $35 for that $5 footlong from Subway, right? Of course not. We can avoid these in two ways: seek out accounts that don't have overdraft fees (usually some buffer, a form of overdraft protection) and negotiating your way out of them.

- **Flexibility.** You want a savings account that lets you easily transfer money into it. If you have a checking account with a bank and are considering opening a savings account with the same bank, make sure that you can easily transfer money between accounts. Many banks will offer perks if you have both types of accounts with them; some will even match small, initial transfers from checking to savings. Having a savings account with a bank indicates that you are willing to commit to a long-term relationship with that bank. They want to keep you, and keep you happy!

CREDIT UNIONS

Credit unions act a lot like banks. You can borrow money from them, make deposits into various kinds of accounts, get checks, wait in line on payday, the works. The inner workings are slightly different though, and this has an impact on the types and quality of service that they provide to members.

I say "member" instead of "customer" because in actuality, people who have accounts at a credit union are owners of the credit union. If you have a checking account at a credit union, you own a small slice of the overall pie. This is different from traditional banks, who merely offer services in exchange for money: at the end of the day, they are trying to make a profit. With a credit union, any money that is made by charging fees or lending money out with interest paid back gets cycled back into the organization. Some credit unions make occasional payments to members, if the credit union has profitable lending and investing practices.

What this means for most people is that credit unions offer lower fees, better customer service, and access to reduced rates on loans. The idea is that the members of a credit union are all working together to create a banking system that works for them, rather than for some fat cat bankers in a far-off city. As a matter of fact, the traditional banking world doesn't really like credit unions, as they tend to offer superior services with fewer strings attached. At the end of the day, though, credit unions are few and far between, and you are just as well served by a good online savings account.

THE BANKS RELOADED

Back in the day, brick and mortar banks were the only real option for consumer banking. You were stuck making deposits and withdrawals within banking hours, and had less flexibility. ATMs got rid of a lot of those limitations, but it wasn't until fairly recently that banking really entered the future and went online entirely. When starting out a new bank account, online banks are a very serious option to consider. This is true for both checking and savings accounts.

There are a few things that make online banking a different, better experience. For one thing, certain online banks have done away with many of the fees associated with banking. They can get away with this because they aren't paying rent on actual buildings or paying staff to manage them. They are cheaper to run, and they make the most of that fact by offering superior service to patrons. Many of them don't try to squeeze every last drop out of you at every turn.

So what should you look for in an online bank?

- Free stuff! Look for banks that offer free checking accounts with no minimum balance requirements that offer things like free bill pay and free checks. Also keep an eye out for free ATM withdrawals. I went to New York City a few times while writing this book and was curious about ATM fees there, so I did some test withdrawals. Some of the ATMs wanted to charge a 9 percent fee! So if I wanted to take out $100, they were expecting me to pay another $9 just to get to my money. No thanks!

- Overdraft protection. The most common type involves having a secondary account linked to the account that you need overdraft protection for. If you overdraw your account by $5, then that $5 is taken out of the back-up account. Usually this is some kind of savings account or a line of credit. So instead of paying the extra $5 plus a $30 fee, you're just paying back the $5 you already spent, and then when you get paid everything goes back to normal. Some online banks have different types of overdraft protection. The 360 Checking account from Capital One, for example, lets you tell the bank that you want them to decline any charges that would overdraw your account. This way you don't end up paying any overdraft fees because the bank simply won't let you overdraw.

- You can get a *lot* of perks if you open a checking and savings account with the same online bank. Sometimes this is a requirement for getting the free stuff.

- Obviously try and get an account that offers you the basics, like an ATM/debit card, the ability to make deposits by transferring from an outside account, and direct deposit.

You'll be happy to hear that online savings accounts tend to pay higher interest rates than traditional ones, for the same reasons they tend to offer better deals when it comes to fees. And some of them have some outstanding features that will make the budgeting practices from our earlier section *much* easier. For example, if you are ready to open a savings account and want to put money aside for a home purchase, a vacation, and an emergency fund, there are a few online savings accounts that will let you divvy up your money into different sections for this exact purposes. You can start three online savings categories within a single account, and direct deposit exactly how much you want into each one. Then, you sit back and watch the balances grow towards your goals!

Here are a few of the online savings accounts that meet a lot of our requirements to get you started:

- **ALLY ONLINE SAVINGS.** This bank generally offers high interest yields. Now, the rates are silly low compared to what was available a few years ago, but anything is better than nothing when it comes to compounding. One of the standout features of Ally is the fantastic online presence. You get live chat, awesome apps, and a streamlined experience from start to finish.

- **360 SAVINGS BY CAPITAL ONE.** One of the top dogs in the online savings world a few years ago was ING Direct Orange. They offered some very high interest rates and a great suite of features. In 2012 this account was converted into the 360 Capital One account, and it is still an excellent option. This account offers some great tools to help you meet your savings goals—and like Ally, it has some top-notch apps.

- **BARCLAYS ONLINE SAVINGS.** In addition to competitive interest rates, this account has no minimum balance requirements or monthly fees. It is also backed by the company's reputation as one of the largest and most stable financial institutions in the world.

DISCLAIMER: *Banks change quite a bit, and the information about specific banks and accounts in this book might be different when you read it. Banks like to merge and change their names, so in a year they might have different policies, names, and who knows what else. But like with the rest of this book, knowing about them and the types of services they offer will give you some great tools on your path to badassery.*

I recommend looking first at online accounts, as opposed to traditional banks and credit unions. They offer so many features, are easily accessible, and will get rid of many of the headaches associated with banking. After figuring out your budget, this is the very next step towards becoming a financial badass. You aren't going to be able to employ the practices in the budgeting section without having the account structure to back them up. Do it sooner rather than later and you will be well on your way. It only takes a few hours to open linked online checking and savings accounts, a few seconds to download the apps, and then a few business days to settle your direct deposits. Once you have that all taken care of, you will be ready to get moving!

ACCOUNT SAFETY AND INSURANCE

You might be wondering whether or not your money is safe in a checking or savings account. I'm sure we all know someone who keeps money in coffee cans buried in the backyard or behind a loose brick in the basement. While this concern for self-preservation is admirable, it definitely isn't necessary! Nearly every bank account in the United States is *insured* against the collapse of the bank by the Federal Deposit Insurance Corporation, or FDIC.

The FDIC was created by Congress way back in the 1930s to help the economy recover from the Great Depression. The FDIC insures many types of accounts up to $250,000. Let's say you have a savings account at a small bank, with $60,000 in it. One night, the bank manager transfers all electronic funds to a gift card, empties the vault, burns the building down, and hops on a plane to Crimea. Thankfully, you aren't out of luck! The FDIC's purpose is to pay out the money lost to customers of the bank up to the limit for each account type, assuming the bank was a participating one.

So, sleep tight, and don't let the bank bugs bite.

MONEY MARKET DEPOSIT ACCOUNTS

The main alternative to the classic checking–savings breakdown of money management accounts is actually a hybrid of the two: a helpful monstrosity that borrows features from both types of accounts to offer something different to customers. This is a money market account—specifically a money market deposit account. Here is how they work.

Money market accounts have more in common with savings accounts than checking accounts. To begin with, you earn interest with them. In fact, the main draw of money market accounts is that they tend to offer higher interest rates than traditional savings accounts. The difference might be very small. For example, when I started writing this book you might see something like 0.33 percent for the MMDA versus 0.09 percent for the savings account. As you will find out, a little bit goes a long way when you are talking about compounding.

MMDAs make up for paying out at a higher interest rate by employing many restrictions. Minimum balance requirements are much higher, and there are typically restrictions on how often you can withdraw money from the account. However, many of these accounts will issue checks and/or a debit card for the account. So, while you may have a limit on the number of withdrawals, you can take the money out more quickly and easily than a traditional savings account. This is where a money market account works kind of like a checking account. Have a look at what sorts of things are available:

- **Ally Bank Money Market Account.** This account offers interest rates competitive with most regular online savings accounts. It also ticks most of the boxes for what we want: no monthly fees, no minimum deposit requirements, and flexibility when it comes to withdrawals and deposits.

- **EverBank.** This account has a high minimum balance requirement but offers high returns as well. There are no monthly fees here either, and you get free ATM withdrawals. This is a great way to kickstart money market savings, if you can take advantage of the high introductory interest rates.

- **Synchrony.** Good rates, the same lack of fees from the above accounts, and a very wide network of ATMs that you can make withdrawals from without paying any fees—and if you do find yourself forced to use an out-of-network ATM, Synchrony will rebate the fees up to a certain amount at the end of each month.

C OF D

Unfortunately, there is no banking-themed *Call of Duty* game. Maybe we will get there some day. In the context of accounts, "C of D" stands for *certificates of deposit*, usually abbreviated to "CDs." CDs are a more complicated way of saving money with a bank. They work sort of like a loan, but in reverse. To open a CD account, you make a deposit, and agree to a fixed amount of time for the account to mature. CDs are *time deposits*, which means that they mature over a specific amount of time, ranging anywhere from a few months to five years. This is the most typical range. While your money is in a CD account, you earn interest. When the time agreement is reached, you can withdraw the money and pocket the interest you earned. They are considered a very stable way of investing your money, and are a class of account protected by FDIC insurance.

Just like MMDAs, CDs carry higher interest rates that come with restrictions. Average rates for one year CDs over the past few years have been around 0.52 percent—much better than what you are looking at for savings accounts, and somewhat higher than most low-tier MMDAs. The larger the principle (the money you put in), the higher your interest rate will be. Additionally, the longer the term you commit to, the higher the interest. The restrictions, however, are more severe than previous accounts we have talked about.

When starting a CD account, the understanding is that you won't touch the money until the end date. If you insist on withdrawing money from one, you will often lose much of your earned interest in penalties.

Since CDs work a bit differently than other accounts, as you have seen, the most important factors here are interest, deposit term length, and minimum balances. You're all going to find yourselves in different financial situations, but if you stick with the principles of minimizing fees, properly allocating your monthly income, and developing the habit of reading the fine print, you can do well with a number of different accounts. Listed next are some example CDs to give you an idea of what they require and how they work for you. You will recognize some of these names from earlier sections.

BANK	INTEREST %	DEPOSIT TERM	MINIMUM BALANCE
Capital One 360	2%	2 years	$1
Barclays	2%	3 years	$1
EverBank	2%	1 year	$5,000
Discover	2%	3 years	$2,500

as of 2018

Let's say you decide to open a Capital One 360 CD (wow that's a mouthful!) and start off the account with $750. In two years, your savings will have gone up to $774.19. That's not a huge gain, but you can see the principle in action. As you will find out in later sections, what may look like a measly 24 bucks can in fact become a source of huge earning potential when we talk about long-term, net-saving for retirement.

This is all well and good, but I want you to take one thing from this little overview of CDs and MMDAs. This is what we like to call "park-in-place" money. That means it is good for a little bump, good to help increase your emergency funds a little bit. They are super conservative, which means they are boring—too boring for you, and too boring for us. It is good that you know about them, but we have bigger and better plans for your money.

THE HOW AND WHY

So, we've gone over some of the "hows" of saving. There are plenty of options, and whether you go with a money market account or traditional savings account, or can afford to tie up your money in a CD, you will earn a little interest. More importantly, you will have set aside money for the "what ifs" of life and begun saving for specific goals, be they a new house, a new car, or that trip to Europe with friends. While these might seem like good reasons for why we save, this isn't the only answer.

Back to our favorite characters, Jack and Jen. They are getting ready to head to college. Jack, inspired by Jen's patience and her sweet ride, did his own research and started a savings account at a local bank. Jen, the budding financial whiz, put some of her savings into a fancy three-year CD that will mature when she is going into her senior year of college. Jack is impressed with her discipline when it comes to saving money today, even though she won't be tapping into it for a few years. He can't help but wonder, since he is the curious type, whether or not there is something more out there. Something that can potentially be used to earn much more. After all, they don't need to use the money right away...

Let's think about this for a second. Should Jack actually be impressed? A CD rate is only slightly higher than many savings accounts, which are at just 0.15 percent a year. This is a rate for the dinosaurs. If you were earning a measly 0.15 percent a year, it would take almost **500 years** to double your money. This is not ambitious enough for us. A CD or savings account earning this kind of money can be useful for an emergency fund, or for shorter term goals like those mentioned earlier. But what if you are saving for later in life, *years* later? And later, you will find out another real-world reason why these types of interest rates just don't cut it: inflation. **Low interest rates have a hard time keeping up with inflation, the general increase in prices over time.**

What if I told you Jen had much more ambitious plans than earning a mere 1 or 1.5 percent? She Googled investments and discovered that they have the potential to earn a much higher rate of return. I'm not talking 2 percent or 5 percent. Try 8 percent, or higher! She put two and two together. 8 percent? That's 16 times higher than a savings account, which only earns .50 percent per year. Think about it this way: If Jen earned 8 percent, and Jack was content with the .50 percent offered by his savings account, it would take him nearly 16 years to have the same ending balance she would have after one year. He had a *wow* moment of his own!

How is this possible? What type of investment could offer returns this high? Other than highly speculative endeavors (like bitcoin) or those that require large upfront capital (like real estate), I mean. It is possible by investing in the stock market, which to many people might seem as hard as learning Greek. *Oh my*, Jack thought, *I don't know anything about stocks. I don't know what they are, how to invest in them, what to invest in, or anything!*

Like Jack, you might be wondering these same things. Yes, we save for houses, trips to Europe, and cars. We save for a rainy day. But if we are interested in even longer-term plans, years or even decades later, there is another reason to save. As our heroes are finding out, *the real purpose of saving money is to invest it.* Since we now understand *why* we save, we are almost ready to talk about *how* such a thing is possible, and how you can grab that amazing 8 percent or higher! But before we get there, let's grab a bite, or get a drink. Not really—I'm talking about spending money! Something we all take pleasure in, and to live and enjoy life, we *must* take part in. I am not going to tell you how to spend your money, or what to spend it on. But there is such a thing as smart spending. As you are about to find out (if you didn't already have a plastic little card) the world runs on credit—it's everywhere and essential to living. Let's learn about credit; let's master it; let's own it!

CHAPTER TWO: SPEND!

Spending money…how fun is that? No matter what it is—a nice watch, a fancy phone, a delicious dinner out on the town (your Instagram isn't going to post on its own, right?), or movie tickets—well, you can certainly spend money on the things you enjoy without having to worry about going broke. We already have a solid base for saving money, and budgeting our monthly income into categories. Now that that's behind us, we can talk about making the most out of our fun money, and not getting in trouble with that plastic card that allows us to buy almost anything!

CREDIT SCORE

I'm sure most of you have seen those free credit report commercials. Guy dresses up like a pirate, sings a stupid song about getting his identity stolen, how his website saved the day, and so on. Well, that particular site is out of business for scamming people, but that's another story.

However, it *is* very important that you know your credit score, for several reasons. Your credit score impacts what rates you get on car loans and a mortgage, what credit cards you have access to, and how likely you are to get a loan for a small business. A good credit score is an indicator of your overall financial health, and it is something you should pay attention to.

WHAT IS IT?

Your credit score is a number, calculated based on several factors, that indicates how trustworthy of a borrower you are. Some of the factors that go into this calculation include:

- Payment history on existing lines of credit
- Length of credit history
- Number of accounts (credit cards/loans)
- Ratio of available credit to balance

Based on these and other variables, certain agencies assign you a credit score, which can range from around 300 to around 850. There are currently four major companies that offer credit scores. These are:

- Experian
- Equifax
- TransUnion
- FICO (Fair Isaac Corporation)

There is some variety when it comes to score specifics, but in general, a score in the 300 to 600 range is considered poor, a score in the 600 to 700 range is considered good, and a score in the 700+ range is excellent.

CHECKING YOUR SCORE

You can find out your score a few different ways. The most official one is the government-mandated free report you are entitled to, from each major credit reporting agency, every 12 months. A credit report contains your credit score, but also details what debts you owe, your credit history, and more. You can get this free report from annualcreditreport.com. Any other website, like the pirate-y one we mentioned up above, is most likely a semi-scam geared towards getting you to sign up for costly identity monitoring, and other services that you probably don't need.

You can also get your credit score as a perk for various checking accounts or credit card lines. For example, Capital One and Discover both have credit score monitoring built into their credit card ecosystems. Checking on it every once in a while certainly can't hurt.

You can also get an aggregate of your score, with limited report information, from online services such as Credit Sesame and CreditKarma. NerdWallet even wraps up credit score tracking, credit card reward overviews, and financial planning and saving content into one online service. There will be resources in the back of this book that will direct you to these various sites and services. Additionally, some banks have started offering credit monitoring and credit score services free as part of checking accounts. When looking to start a checking account, this is something to keep in mind, as it is a nice perk!

HOW DO I GET A GOOD SCORE?

Getting and maintaining a good credit score is going to vary a little for everyone, but there are a few good rules of thumb that you can follow to keep your score high:

* Pay your bills on time! This is one of the great rules for everything finance-related. Pay your bill on time. Pay early. Pay extra.

* Keep balances low, at 15 percent or 25 percent of the credit limit. If you have a $10,000 credit limit, try and keep your balance around $2,000. Generally, the higher the balance is relative to the credit limit, the more your credit score will hurt.

* Don't be afraid to keep credit lines open. Having a good credit score is all about being an attractive borrower. Creditors want to lend to people who appear trustworthy, but they also want people to use their line of credit. So, keeping a low balance rather than *no* balance isn't necessarily a bad thing.

THE IMPORTANCE OF BUILDING CREDIT, AND WHY A CREDIT SCORE IS A BIG DEAL

Building credit is the idea that slowly, through borrowing, spending, and repaying money, you establish a certain amount of trustworthiness as a borrower. When you borrow money, whether it be in the form of a credit card, student loan, or mortgage, you are telling the world, "Hey, I am a stable investment. You can lend me money, I will do something productive with it, then pay you back, plus interest." It is very important nowadays to establish yourself this way, because the better your credit score and history, the more doors will open for you. If you want to buy a house, the size of the down payment is often linked to your credit. When you want to take out a student loan, your credit will determine whether you need to go through the hassle of finding a cosigner. Some apartments even have restrictions on tenancy when it comes to credit score and history.

Our entire economy runs on the lending of money. Governments do it, businesses do it, colleges and universities do it, and private citizens do it. Like it or not, having good credit is necessary in the modern world. An important part of your financial health will begin with establishing credit early, and keeping it in good shape. Later, we'll go over what to look for when choosing a credit card, as this is the easiest way to dive in the water and get established.

#NOTMYDEBT

Financial badasses turn the tables on debt. They make the most of credit card rewards, special promotions, one-time deals, and Cyber Monday. They make credit card companies shake their heads, wondering where they went wrong.

Maybe you have heard about the Chase Sapphire card? It was what they like to call a "premium" credit card. Sounds cool, doesn't it? Well, it was, because the rewards for using the card were really, really good. So good, in fact, that enough dangerous folks (lookin' at you) tapping into those rewards caused Chase to drastically cut back on things like sign-up bonuses. Rather than making bank off consumers, badass consumers were making bank off *them*.

What do we say to the standards of old debt? Not today. With a universe of information at your fingertips and knowing what's controllable, you understand that debt isn't a bad thing. You don't need to worry about some asshole bursting through the door to break your kneecaps trying to get his shit back.

So the point is, turn the tides and harness the power of debt to work for you instead of against you. Think of debt like a tool, just like (almost) anything else. You can use a hammer to drive in a nail or you can use it to test the latest Gorilla Glass. Don't freak out if you owe $2,000 to credit card companies. Stay calm, and pay on. Meet your monthly (and then some) and watch your credit score rise (and your limit!). That is, as they say, priceless.

A financial badass knows how to do the things that she wants without having to worry. She understands priorities. She knows there is no one-size-fits-all solution to, well, anything.

She and you have flexibility. So do the work, be safe, and have a ton of fun in the meantime.

IN YOUR ACCORD DOING DONUTS...

Buying a car is going to be a big part of most of your lives. Depending on where you live, cars can be anywhere from a minor convenience to an absolute necessity. Getting a car isn't cheap, either, so you will need to be prepared when making the decision. There is a lot to consider— make and model, year, number of miles, maintenance, and so on.

The first rule of thumb I am going to give you is this: if you are under 25, or buying your first car, you might not want to buy a new one! You will end up paying too much for something that loses a ton of value as soon as you drive it off the lot. Think about it this way: if you buy a car for $8,000, new, then as soon as you drive away with it, it is worth only $6,000. A few years later, it is worth, say, $4,000. You can see where this is going, right? You're just bleeding money, especially if you end up selling the car when you haven't gotten the most out of it. If you plan on driving a new car until the thing falls apart on the road in 10 or 15 years, then maybe a new car is right for you. But only a few of

G$TIP: Try cargurus.com to f
out if you're getting a good deal

you are buying cars with that kind of foresight, and you shouldn't *have* to. New cars also cost more to insure, so you are paying a premium on a monthly basis just for the privilege of driving around in a new ride.

So, let's talk about making a smart used car purchase. The first step is to decide what you need. Do you need space to haul stuff, maybe for work? Do you need space for tools? Are you driving long distances for work, or are you going to be pretty light on the car? What are gas prices like in your area, and how much can you afford to pay for gas? These sorts of questions will help you decide on features you need, and then we can go on to the next step: settling on a budget. This would be a good time to flip back to the first chapter and look at the budgeting advice there.

Most car purchases are made through a loan. Some other party (the car dealership or a bank) gives you a loan for the amount of the car purchase, and then you pay back the loan. It works for the most part like a mortgage or student loan. You will have to pay interest. So when we talk about budgeting a car purchase, what we are talking about is deciding how much of your monthly income you can commit to car payments. You got a glimpse of this when we learned about budgeting in the first chapter. I am going to keep it simple for you: **keep your monthly car payments below 15 percent of your monthly income.** I would like to say 10 percent, but that just might not be possible for a lot of you. Deciding ahead of time what amount you are willing to pay each month for a car is a key step in the process. When in doubt, 10 percent, 20 percent, 30 percent, 40 percent!

So, you have figured out your use case, what you need in a car, and your budget, and you are ready to start shopping. There are plenty of places to start looking, some of the most popular places being CarMax centers and the used division of new car dealerships. I would suggest sticking with reputable places like this, as they have to meet certain requirements to sell used cars. In a nutshell, you run a very low risk of being scammed! You can look for a car on Craigslist, but that might be too much to chew for a first car purchase. When you head to a dealership, explain your situation to the dealer and work with them to find something that suits your needs.

Once you have some information, look up reviews of the cars that you have narrowed down the field to. Look at reports of reliability, typical maintenance issues, and the longevity of the car. Look online for prices so you can see if you are getting a good deal. Once you feel armed by your homework, you are ready to buy a car. Make sure you get a mechanic inspection on the car you pick before you sign on the dotted line; most car dealerships will let you do this. You were made for this!

CHOOSING A CAR INSURANCE VENDOR

If you thought there were a lot of options for buying a used car, you ain't seen nothin' yet! Settling on an insurance provider puts them all to shame. I don't have the space (or the desire, to be honest!) to analyze all the options, but here are a few pointers that will narrow down the field to vendors that will provide you good service at a reasonable price.

Just like with the car-buying process, the insurance-buying one begins with you deciding what you want. Do you want the cheapest insurance possible? Do you want a lot of protection? Something in between? The answers to these questions are tied in with your use case identified above. If you rely on your car a lot (for example, if you work at a different job site a few times a week and have to travel many different distances) you might want to pay a little bit extra in order to protect your important investment. If you drive infrequently, you can probably get away with cheaper insurance. Once you decide on what class of service best suits you based on how you use your car, take a look at these factors:

- ☛ A good stat is to pick an insurance provider that is legally allowed to operate in your state! You can find a list of registered providers on the Department of Insurance's website for your state.

- Look at reviews of the provider. This should be easy for you; if you have ever bought something off Amazon, you are already skilled at parsing product reviews!

- Make sure you compare *several* providers. Don't just go with the first one you see; make sure you compare rates.

- If you already have insurance and are looking again at your service, make sure you report any reductions in mileage or usage. Any changes in your driving patterns that reduce your risk as a driver can usually be turned into reduced rates.

- Look for perks that set some providers apart from others. For example, some companies offer reduced rates for people with good driving records. If you are young, you are going to be paying more than most for insurance; every dollar you can save will be worth it!

- Make sure you know what repair centers your insurer will send you to if you do get into an accident. Make sure they can work on your vehicle, and check and see what quality of service they provide (for example, do they have good reviews? Do they prefer off-brand replacement parts or parts directly from the car manufacturer?)

- Or, just take the easy way out and hire an insurance agent to do all of this for you! There may even be discounts for bundling home and auto insurance together!

Setting a budget for car insurance isn't nearly as stressful as settling on a budget for car payments. The average American pays less than $1,000 a year in car insurance; with that in mind, shoot for monthly insurance payments of between $75 and $150 a month. What prices are available to you are largely out of your control, even though you can shop around and try to get a better deal. Your age, sex, driving history, and credit score are going to be some of the main factors that decide your rate, and these cannot be changed overnight, or at all. So work with what you have, and be diligent in the research phase of the shopping journey.

SAVING AND SPENDING AND COLLEGE

One of the largest financial decisions young people (and not so young!) face today is whether or not to pursue education. On one hand, getting a degree opens innumerable doors professionally. On the other, it's very often incredibly expensive. Historically, the value of a college degree has changed dramatically. Gone are the days where you could get a job at a car factory with just a high school education, receive on-the-job training, make a living wage, buy a house, and retire with a comfortable pension. Those sorts of jobs hardly exist, and there are very few of them. For many career paths, a college degree is the key that opens the door to success, and the only way forward.

Tuition rates have skyrocketed in recent years. In 1976, the average tuition and fees for a private four-year institution were around $10,000. You were looking at paying $40,000 in total for an undergraduate degree. By 2000, this number had topped $20,000 per year, and by the time of this book, the average yearly rate was around $33,000. This isn't even counting room and board.

The sad reality is, the costs of higher education have significantly outpaced salary changes over the past few decades. Adjusted for inflation (there goes that word again), we actually don't make that much more money now than we did in the 1960s and 1970s. So while college prices have gone through the roof, earnings have stagnated. In fact, we make less money now, on average, than we did in 1999! This means that would-be students today are faced with a difficult dilemma: college degrees are more and more in demand in the modern workplace, but they have outrun our ability to pay for them.

Why college costs have gone up so much is a complicated story. It has to do partly with the fact that many more Americans today want to go to college than back in the 1960s and 1970s. To accommodate the rise in the student population, colleges and universities have had to charge more. Another reason is the fact that school administrations have grown. Institutions have added more administrative positions than they have faculty by a wide margin. Whether this is to line their pockets or not doesn't really matter. The rise in tuition costs is beyond the scope of this book; we just need to deal with the reality of paying for college!

Enter student loans. With no ability to earn enough to pay for a college education, we have ended up borrowing our way to graduation instead. This isn't to say that student loans are new thing; they have actually been around in some form or another since the 1950s, when the federal government first offered loans to students pursuing certain kinds of degrees. They have truly built up steam in the last 30 years or so. The student loan companies figured out the trend in rising college costs, and they capitalized on it admirably.

Generally speaking, student loans fall into two broad categories: federal loans and private loans. There are some very important differences between them that will heavily influence how you pay for college if you must take out loans.

FEDERAL LOANS	PRIVATE LOANS
Some federal loans have amount limits. The Perkins loan, for example, caps at $5,500 per year, and Stafford loans cap at $5,500 to $10,500 per year, depending on student status.	There are typically no limits to private student loan amounts. The issuing companies are happy to loan you as much as possible.
All payments are deferred until after graduation. There is also typically a grace period, where no payments are required for a six month period after graduation while you find a job.	Many private loan companies insist that payments begin while you are still a student.
While you are a student, the government pays off the interest accumulated on most loans. After graduation, you become liable for the interest. If your loan payments are deferred, the government pays interest then as well. These are known as *subsidized* loans.	Interest begins accruing from day one, and you have to pay it all back. Lenders will never pay off your interest for you.

Interest rates for federal student loans are fixed; you are locked in for the life of the loan to whatever rate is in place when you take out the loan. These loans have relatively low interest rates.

Interest rates for private student loans are variable, which means that based on the overall performance of the economy, the issuing entity can raise or lower interest rates as they see fit. Some private student loan interest rates can become insurmountable, getting as high as 15 percent and beyond.

The federal government forgives some loans based on certain criteria, like becoming a teacher, becoming disabled, or performing public service.

Private student loans are almost never forgiven. You will be responsible for paying off the loan forever, even if you declare bankruptcy.

If you are out of work or experiencing hardship, there are several options in place to help. You can apply for a *deferment,* which delays your payments temporarily. During deferment, the federal government pays interest that accumulates on the loan. You can also apply for a *forbearance* if you don't qualify for a deferment, which grants a (typically) twelve month period where payments can be put off or reduced. While in forbearance, interest still accumulates on your loan.

Private student loans (are you seeing a pattern yet?) are almost never deferred or put into forbearance. Lenders expect to be paid, and they are very reluctant to grant leniency on payment plans unless you are well into your payment schedule and have developed a relationship with the lender.

The student loan system has ballooned out of control, and there is currently $1.48 trillion in outstanding student loan debt. Trillion with a T! This is more than outstanding credit card debt, and more than outstanding car and small business loans. Student debt is the second largest source of household debt, behind housing loans. An *absurd* amount of money is owed to the federal government and private lenders, and time will tell if borrowers will ever be able to get out from under the weight of their loans in an increasingly cutthroat and demanding job market.

Put simply, **private student loans generally aren't worth it.** You don't want to get hustled, and as Einstein will shortly explain... you want to be on the earning end of compounding, not the paying end! Given the nearly night-and-day comparison, it's no surprise that in 2017, 72 percent of student loan borrowers used only federal loans, 5 percent used only private loans, and 22 percent used both. They *certainly* shouldn't be the primary way you pay for college. The interest rates are bad, the borrower privileges are negligible, and in all likelihood you will be saddled with them for far longer than you need to be. If you must take out private loans, keep them as small as possible.

LOAN CONSOLIDATION

One of the biggest tools you have when dealing with student loans is the consolidation process. When consolidating a loan, you take out a *new* loan for the amount of your existing loans. This new loan (usually from a new vendor) pays off the old loans. This offers many benefits, not the least of which is the fact that you bring several different loans under one, making monthly payments a little more manageable. Very often, consolidation lenders offer very attractive terms to graduates, since they are eager for business. Consolidated loans often have low interest rates and lower monthly payments. This ends up extending the life of the loan, which means that you have more cash on a day-to-day basis after consolidating at the cost of paying more over the total life of the loan. On top of that, the interest rates for consolidated loans are usually *fixed*, which means that what you see is what you get. If you consolidate and get an interest rate of 4 percent (not uncommon, and really good!) and it is fixed, you never have to worry about that number going up due to market fluctuations or anything like that.

Consolidating your loans is a good idea in most circumstances. The only times you *don't* want to go this route are if you are either very close to paying off your loans, or if you have built up a good enough relationship with your existing lender and have access to forbearance periods and low interest rates, for example. Consolidation is a fairly complicated process when it comes to paperwork, but the barrier to entry is very low (credit score generally has no impact on eligibility, and there is no maximum limit to the amount you can consolidate) and the perks are almost always worth it! As is so often the case, each situation is different and there is no one-size-fits-all loan consolidation process.

FAFSA

No, I didn't fall asleep on my keyboard. A FAFSA is a real thing! FAFSA stands for *Free Application for Federal Student Aid*. This is a form filled out by prospective or current college students that takes into account income, bank account information, and other variables to determine your eligibility for federal student aid. If you want a federal loan or grant to pay for college, you *need* to fill out FAFSA.

It is very important that you take care of this as soon as possible. FAFSA forms can be filled out and turned in for a certain amount of time before the academic year, and aid is awarded on a first-come, first-served basis. Do it *early*. In 2016, FAFSA forms could be turned in starting October 1st. Do it the first day. Your education is incredibly important, and you need to be sure you get the most out of the many resources the federal government has made available to students. And don't forget, you will need to fill out FAFSA *every* year you plan on enrolling in school. It can all be done online!

To make the process of filling out FAFSA hassle-free and quick, make sure you have the following information before you head to fafsa.ed.gov:

- Your Social Security number.
- Most recent W-2, tax return, or other proofs of income.
- Bank statements and investment statements.
- A FAFSA ID, which you can get through the website.

With all of this under our belt, let's consider what the implications are for the modern student. Going too far into debt will severely hamper our ability to invest in retirement, and anyone with over $100,000 in student loan debt is going to be on somewhat shaky financial ground. So how do we achieve our goal of getting a higher education, which will drastically improve our future earning potential, without getting in over our heads with debt, which will eat right through the fruit of that potential?

The first big way you can shake off the threat of crippling student debt is to consider going to a public college or university. These are schools that receive the bulk of their budget from some combination of state and national funding. Public colleges and universities are ways for our government to subsidize the education and improvement of citizens. They offer incredibly high-quality education...and they are much, much cheaper than private schools.

Most public universities are "state schools," which means they are funded by state and local governments. Because of this, they offer reduced tuition rates to students who are residents of whichever state funds the school. These reduced rates are a great benefit. Let's look at exactly how much you can save by going to a state school when you reside in that state:

SCHOOL	IN-STATE TUITION (YEARLY)	OUT-OF-STATE TUITION (YEARLY)
University of Maryland	$25,742	$47,606
Clemson University	$25,160	$45,042
Penn State University	$34,778	$50,006
Texas Tech University	$25,776	$38,226
UCLA	$34,844	$62,858

as of 2018

As you can see, the cost difference can be huge. There is some variation, as not all schools have the same policies or pricing structure. Some will be more generous to students based on the quirks of their funding. But the fact remains, public universities and colleges are much more affordable for in-state students. Don't start applying anywhere before you take a thorough look at your state's schools; you can thank me later!

Even though state schools might offer a more attractive financial option, many people have their hearts set on specific programs or degrees offered at private schools. There is also a certain amount of power in a name...who doesn't want to enter the workforce as a Harvard or Princeton graduate? If this is your decision, know what you are getting into before you sign your loan paperwork. Since federal loan limits aren't high enough to pay for a full private university education, you may need to make up the difference with scholarships, grants, and private student loans, or the oldest and still most popular way of paying for higher education: family!

IF AT FIRST YOU DON'T SUCCEED, TRY A HUNDRED MORE TIMES

The internet age has made it incredibly easy to seek out ways to get money for college. If you have an internet connection, you have thousands of scholarship applications at your fingertips. There are websites (scholarships.com...who would have guessed that?) that aggregate thousands of scholarships, and from there you can start a list of those you think you can get. Be diligent. Know the deadlines, GPA requirements, and essay requirements beforehand. Scholarships are competitive, especially with more and more people applying for college, so you want to act quickly and get your applications in ASAP. And remember, you won't get any scholarships you don't apply for...and you lose nothing by applying for them. It's a win-win.

MORE FREE MONEY!

So, you've been accepted to the college of your dreams. Your parents are able to pay some of your tuition, and you got some federal loans as well. You got a scholarship from a local organization in your hometown, and just need a little bit more cold hard cash. Thankfully (or miraculously!) you have made it this far in this book, and know that private student loans are to be avoided if possible. What to do?

Turns out there are other ways to get free money besides scholarships that have to be individually applied for: grants. These come, like loans and scholarships and schools, in many different flavors. The Pell Grant is one of the best options for this type of student. The Pell Grant is a chunk of money that the federal government has made available to students in financial need, a status that is determined by the information you put in your FAFSA. If you meet the requirements, you can get up to $5,815 per year in money for college that doesn't have to be repaid.

There are many other federal grants available. There are grants set aside for veterans and National Guard members, students with disabilities, and students who choose certain career paths. For example, the Academic Competitiveness and SMART (National Science and Mathematics Access to Retain Talent) grants are made available to undergraduate students who decide to major in various math and science sectors. Did you ever see those commercials on TV featuring a guy in a suit covered in dollar signs, running around and yelling? Well, his antics were justified, and he was right! There is a *ton* of free money available for all sorts of things, and paying for a college education is one of the best examples. Included in the back of this book are several resources that you can use to see what grants are available, and what their requirements are.

@RICHKIDSOFINSTAGRAM

A financial badass can buy whatever she wants. I was going to add "within reason" there, but I decided against it. After all, that is subjective. Don't put arbitrary limits on yourself based on what other people say. You work hard, you own what you work for, and you have earned the right and the ability to buy whatever you freaking want. Think big, dream bigger!

Don't worry about things the way generations past did; almost everything changes from one to the other. What was unthinkable 25 years ago is now commonplace. You have options no one else in history has ever had. Would you rather own a house and stay rooted in one place, or go wandering, taking in new places and experiences constantly? Or maybe you want to be rich enough to travel, and buy a house in each city you visit (or just AirBnB it)? Go for it! You get one shot at this thing called life. #yolo

Do and buy what makes you happy. If a house would make you happy, go get one. If what makes you happy is a year of Instagram-worthy eats and drinks, then do that.

Just prepare. Be smart, the way you are in other aspects of your life. You pay attention to your appearance, right? You don't wake up in the morning and think, *Man, I really feel like going out into the world looking like shit.* Of course not. You look good and you feel good.

You curate a social media empire. You choose your hashtags more carefully than I ever could. So why should you give any less attention to your financial life?

Being a financial badass is about knowing the rules well enough to break them, covering your ass while filling your life with swag, and not having to apologize for being too smart for the system.

"Learn the rules like a pro,
so you can break them like an artist."

—Pablo Picasso

WELCOME TO MY CRIB

Many of you might be considering buying a house or a condo in the near future. While the current generation is buying fewer and fewer houses, it is still a very common first big purchase. Buying a house can be very tricky, but when done properly, it can provide a certain quality of life that differs from renting an apartment. On top of that, a house can be seen as a type of investment, one that many in previous generations relied on to see them partially through their retirements.

Buying a house is a big decision. By making it, you're at the very least considering staying in the same area for a while. This is a long-term commitment, so make sure you have a good grasp on the costs—both initial ones and those that come down the road in the form of maintenance and property taxes. Before I talk about this spending category, let's go over some terminology first.

Almost no one buys a house out of pocket, which is to say with money they have sitting in an account somewhere. If you have $300,000 at age 25 to buy a house, chances are you are doing all right and you're definitely the exception. But for most people, the way to buy a house is through a loan called a "mortgage." Keeping it simple, if you find a house you are ready to buy, you approach a bank or other lender with the cost and information about the house, and they will give you a loan to buy it.

Mortgages, since they are so large, typically come with a long repayment period. The most common and popular repayment plans occur over twenty-five or thirty years. Towards the beginning of this period, your monthly payments will mostly go towards accumulated interest. Over time, the interest that builds will be less and less as the principle gets paid off. Some lenders might give you the option to make interest-only payments if you are having a hard time making the full payment. This can be helpful in a pinch, but it is important to remember that you will have to get around to paying the principle one day, so don't agree to an interest-only plan unless you absolutely have to.

We talked early in the saving section about how to budget for a mortgage payment, and there were a few tips on the home-buying process. There are a million books that cover everything from searching for to evaluating and buying a house, which are beyond the scope of this book. The last thing to cover here is yet another cost associated with the typical American Dream of owning your own home.

THERE'S ALWAYS A TAX!

I'm talking about property tax. It isn't enough that you paid a ton of money to buy a house, you also need to pay the government a tax for "using" the land the house is on. (Damn, some of those government people are geniuses!) Property taxes are one of the main ways both the state and federal government make money. They are primarily calculated based on the value of your property. You will have to pay your property taxes once a year.

Thankfully, you don't have to necessarily budget ahead of time and try to predict what your property taxes might be. You can use your mortgage as a way to pay them. If you want to go this route, you will need to have an *escrow account* attached to your mortgage. "Escrow" is definitely a weird word, but all it refers to is an account that holds money dedicated to paying off certain things. If you have this type of account with your mortgage, your lender will increase your mortgage payment a little bit, and the extra money will go into a fund that, when the time comes, can be used to pay your property taxes. Lenders do this because if you don't pay your mortgage and get foreclosed on, *they* are responsible for any outstanding property taxes. They certainly don't want to cover your ass. This definitely simplifies the process, but know that in 30 years (sounds like forever, I know!) you will have to pay property taxes on your own once you pay off your mortgage.

CALL ME ON MY CELL PHONE

It is hard to come up with a more essential tool for day-to-day life, socially and professionally. You need one, you want one, you have one. There are emails to send, filters to apply to your umpteenth selfie—and as you'll find out later, there are some *dangerous* tools you can use to invest that require a cell phone. So, you have to buy one, and there are a million options. How can we make buying phones and apps a process that doesn't break our saving structure? Just think: without a cell phone, there would be no Snapchat.

There is a pretty common pitfall when it comes to getting a mobile device, and it is the subsidized device trap. I'm sure you have seen it. Apple has an announcement with a questionable musical act, announces the iPhone 47, and then you zip on over to Verizon's website or Amazon to order one. Look at that, it's only $199 up front! What a bargain! And in no time at all, it is plopped perfectly on your doorstep.

Unfortunately, it's not actually a bargain. There are many hidden costs to getting a phone this way, and they have to do with the two-year contract model that is thankfully almost dead. Here is how it worked up until a year or two ago: you buy the phone for $199, then sign a two-year contract. That contract requires you to pay for a certain level of service plan, which is an inflated monthly fee that covers the cost of the *rest* of the device. So over the life of the plan, you are actually paying much more than the cost of the device + service. Customers got wise to this scheme, and carriers have been moving towards a *leasing* model.

On some level, this is another trap. What happens in this kind of plan is you pay an upfront amount (usually pretty low) and then pay an extra amount each month on top of service so that you pay off the remainder of the device's cost. You don't end up paying as much as you would with the previous two-year contract model (and aren't stuck with a contract with heavy cancellation fees), but you are still a bit limited. For example, if you want to change carriers on this type of plan, you are still stuck owing the existing carrier for the difference in cost between what you paid up front plus your number of monthly payments subtracted from the total cost of the device. So let's look at options. There are three main ones:

- You can buy your phone up front, for full price. This means going to Apple or Google and buying the phone for full price directly from them. You then *own* the device completely. You are not leasing it from a carrier. You can switch carriers every week, if you want to. You are free! This is the best option if you anticipate moving frequently, or want to use your phone for a long time. The initial cost will be higher, but you'll save money in the long run.

- You can get a leasing plan that lets you upgrade early. Lots of people want to get the latest and greatest phone each year when new models come out. A few years ago, this made quite a bit of sense, since phones were jumping forward technologically in leaps and bounds. Nowadays, premium phones are incredibly powerful, and can be used for years. A top-flight phone from Apple or Samsung, for example, is going to be crazy fast and powerful for much longer than a year. If you go with an early upgrade lease, you are basically renting a phone for a certain amount of time and paying extra each month, with the ability to trade in your phone for a newer one each year or so. It's very much like leasing a car. It'll cost a little more, but if you always want the latest and greatest, it works.

🍀 Standard leasing is the last option. In this kind of plan, you pay very little up front, lease the phone until it is paid off, then you own it. If you want to keep your phone for a while and see yourself sticking with your carrier, this makes sense. The best part is that, unlike the early-upgrade option, your cell phone bill will actually go *down* after you have finished paying off the device!

If money is no problem: buy your phone outright. You will have the most freedom, and will save money in the long run. You won't be stuck with a carrier, you won't be stuck having to pay extra each month, and if you purchase a high-end phone, you will be set with an awesome device for years. You can still do all the things you want to do; you just added a touch of frugality.

MICRO TRANSACTIONS; OR, REMEMBER WHEN YOU COULD BUY A FULL GAME?

Mobile gaming has taken the world by storm. Phones are getting more powerful, which means they have better and better-looking games all the time. Unfortunately, the guys behind the curtain have figured out that the best way to make money is to offer a free game, and then hide in-app purchases to get people to slowly spend more and more money to keep up with the competition. I'm definitely not going to tell you stop gaming (you could end up being a star player), but I will advise you to be careful when spending money on these kinds of games. A few dollars here and there will really add up, and can even turn into a kind of addiction. Clash of Clans is a pretty good example. To keep up with the other players playing the game, you basically need to buy various in-game currencies to speed up the building of your base. Check out games that have a one-time cost, and have the fully developed experience.

DID YOU KNOW?

Today there are over 180 million people worldwide who watch eSports competitions at least once a month—more than twice as many as in 2012.

IF YOU MUST...

Most paid apps aren't that expensive—a few bucks at the most. There are a few tricks to getting even these for free, though, so before you pull the trigger on buying something, check out these options!

One of the best ways to get free money for apps is Google Opinion Rewards (this obviously only works on Android). When you sign up, you give Google some basic information about yourself. From then on, you periodically get short surveys to fill out that will give you anywhere from a few cents to a dollar in Google credit that you can use to buy games, rent movies, and more. Occasionally you will get a survey that won't pay anything, but don't let that get to you. Someone made over $70 in less than a year just spending a few seconds answering surveys. True story. Google is clever, though, and will sometimes send you trick surveys to make sure you aren't trying to game the system. If you answer one of these trick questions dishonestly, you might not get any more surveys. So just be honest, and watch your balance rise.

Let's say you have earned $10 in survey rewards and want to buy some apps. There is another way you get more for less, on top of your free cash. This involves keeping an eye on what apps and movies and songs are on sale. App developers on both the Google and Apple app stores periodically put apps on sale. Sometimes an app will go from $4.99 to $0.50, or even free! There are a number of places that keep track of app deals, so you can stay on top of things and be ready to snatch up cheap or free stuff. Check out the CheapCharts program for Apple, or the Google Play deals subreddit on Reddit.

GOT ANY MORE OF THEM FREE APPS?

With a bit of digging, you can get a *ton* of free or cheap software that is normally very expensive. The key for a lot of these is being a student, or at least having a valid student email. For example, did you know that Microsoft offers nearly the entire Office suite for free to students? If you have a .edu email address, point your browser of choice to Microsoft's Office 365 website, and viola, free software! You can also get steep discounts on Photoshop, VM Ware, AutoCad, and more as a student or teacher. You can also get reduced pricing and a free introductory period for Amazon Prime. I can't possibly go into *all* of the stuff you can snag for less than the usual price, but a quick Google search will send you on your way.

THE "WHY" OF SPENDING

At the end of chapter one, we talked about the why of saving. It is a simple one to remember: because we need to! While there are shorter-term reasons for saving for needs and desires, **we are saving long-term in order to invest.** Remember the freedom fund idea from earlier in the book? Having short-term financial freedom is great and all, but to be truly badass we want to extend that financial freedom into future years. With the question of saving answered, we can turn our attention to the "why" of spending.

It might seem as if the counterpart question here is, "Why do we spend?" Good question, but not the important one! We spend because we need and want things; clothes, food, PlayStations, cocktails. The real question here is, "Why should we spend *smartly?*" The tips and tricks in this chapter encourage you to spend carefully and smartly, so that you have more money to save, which means you have more money to invest. This is just as easy to remember: **we spend wisely in order to invest more.**

Think about it this way. Spending money, as we talked about in the first chapter, is the end goal. Money is a means to that end. Along the way, you have to make many little saving and spending decisions so that you can make the most of your ability to spend after retiring (man, that is a nasty term!). And as you will find out in the next chapter, long-term investing (primarily in a retirement plan) is the best way to maximize your future spending potential. At the end of the day, everything in these first two chapters is the pre-game party, and the real show is about to begin. It's where we learn about that alien technology: the stock market. I told you earlier I was saving the best for last, and we have arrived! Let's get f-ing rich!

CHAPTER THREE: INVEST!

This is the longest chapter in this book, and for good reason. We're going to cover a wide range of topics, from how to invest in the stock market to why you should even bother with stocks at all. We've covered analyzing your monthly income and good practices when it comes to saving and spending money. These tools will see you through day-to-day living, and we are now ready to look forward to the future. This is the *really* fun part of the book, but by no means will you become an expert in the next hour or so of reading the pages in front of you. The beautiful thing is, you don't *have* to become an expert or know everything. Just knowing the basics and a few fundamentals will set you well on your way towards becoming a badass.

> INVESTING IS AN ACTIVITY IN WHICH CONSUMPTION TODAY IS FOREGONE IN AN ATTEMPT TO ALLOW GREATER CONSUMPTION AT A LATER DATE.
>
> *Berkshire Hathaway Shareholder Letter, 2017*

INVESTMENT VOCAB (BORING, BUT BEAR WITH ME)

Before getting into the magic of compounding, we should familiarize ourselves with some of the financial instruments that make up the investing world. Now, these next few pages are a little slow, so you will have to bear with me. It's not that tough and it's not that long, but unfortunately Selena Gomez isn't going to pop out of this book (à la *The Big Short*) and break down the subject for you from behind a blackjack table (now *that* would be magic!) As you will find out, 401(k)s and similar vehicles are powered from within by stocks, bonds, and mutual funds. Let's look at each of these.

Stocks

Shares of stock are essentially little slices of a company. They can be acquired in various ways, and function in various ways. The thing to bear in mind is that they represent ownership of a company or equity. "Stock" refers to a general ownership of a company through shares, which are individual certificates of ownership. Did you ever see *Wolf of Wall Street*? If not, watch it tonight; it's awesome! Well, Jordan Belfort (Leonardo DiCaprio's character) misrepresented to investors the nature of the company whose stock they were buying from him. He bought the stock at a low price, artificially inflated the value by sweet-talking his marks, and then sold it at a much higher price knowing the investors would never get anything out of it. From there it was all Quaaludes, sports cars, and jail.

For example, let's say you own a share of Apple. This doesn't just mean you have a piece of paper with some cash value attached to something related to Apple; you actually *own* a small part of the company. It might just be 0.00001 percent of the company, but you own it nonetheless. That is pretty cool! And if Apple does well and their value goes up, the value of your share does as well.

Stocks can be very volatile, especially in the short term, which means their value can go up or down based on more things than we can list. Really, it can be anything from a company's earnings to the weather. They can be hard to predict, but based on certain factors, some can be more stable than others. This will be important later when we discuss the role stocks play in a 401(k) and other long-term savings vehicles.

HOW CAN I BUY STOCK?

Unless you walked into a bookstore for this book (or are reading it on your Kindle), odds are you ordered it online. Maybe it was even an Amazon Prime purchase. Even more likely, you ordered it on your phone—something that has gone from being cool to being convenient to being *necessary*!

So, we know that stocks represent equity in a company. Equity means ownership—how would you like to become an owner of Amazon?!

"YES!" you say. *"How do I do it?"*

There are multiple ways. If you just gotta own that stock now (in true Prime fashion), download an app and get buying. Schwab Mobile, TD Ameritrade, E-Trade Mobile (the ones with the awesome commercials), and RobinHood are just a few available. Load money into the apps (you can even deposit checks straight into your phone) and *voilà*—you're in business!

Bonds

A bond is a type of loan. There are many types, depending on who is issuing them. The federal government issues bonds, as do private companies. When you buy a bond, you are loaning the issuing body that money. You then get interest from the entity you bought the bond from, and then ultimately the bond value is paid back years later, depending on the term of the bond. Bonds are considered more stable investments than stocks. They are usually quite predictable, and certain things like the interest rate and date you will be repaid are always known. A good portion of any portfolio, including investment portfolios, should be made up of bonds. They certainly aren't as sexy as stocks can be, and may not get you to where you want to be as quickly, but even a get-rich-slow scheme can make you rich!

Just before this section, we talked about how owning shares in a company means you own a bit of the company itself. Bonds can work in a similar way. Let's use Apple again; imagine they are building a new plant to help with the production of the next iPhone, and they want to raise money to fund the plant by issuing bonds. You can buy those bonds, making you a *bondholder* of Apple's debt. Owning a bond means you own a bit of Apple's debt, just like owning a share means you own a bit of Apple as a company. So now, Apple owes you money! Don't worry, you will be paid; you will receive quarterly dividends until the bond term is over, assuming Apple is in business and remains "solvent" (a fancy word that just means they can pay their debts).

Mutual Funds

Google tells me the definition of a mutual fund is, "an investment program funded by shareholders that trades at diversified holdings and is professionally managed." Yikes. It's a start, anyway! Investopedia has it a bit better: "A mutual fund is an investment vehicle made up of a pool of funds collected from many different investors for the purposes of investing in securities such as stocks, bonds, money market instruments, and similar assets." Mutual funds are extremely popular and are the dominant way to invest in stocks and bonds found in retirement plans today. In fact, more than $4 trillion (yes, that says "trillion") is invested in mutual funds in America.

Think of a mutual fund as a collection (called a "portfolio") made up of the stocks and bonds we just talked about, put together and managed as one package by an investment firm. Professionals manage mutual funds for the most part, and if you invest in one you won't be meddling with the fund on a daily basis. The firms that offer mutual funds know what they are doing, and this means that mutual funds are a good way for smaller investors (i.e., you!) to play in the "big leagues" and become powerful investors.

There are many types of mutual funds. **Bond funds**, as you might expect, focus on bonds: either safe, fixed-income bonds or low-value bonds bought low and sold high. Some **specialty mutual funds** concentrate on stocks and bonds in specific industries: health, agriculture, finance, aerospace, etc. But the majority of mutual funds invest primarily in stocks, and these are called **equity funds**. Different equity funds will focus on stocks in companies with specific features, like growth potential or established quality. There are over 8,000 mutual funds available, and we certainly aren't going to go through them all here! The point is that mutual funds can be a very powerful investing tool, and they are varied and popular for a reason.

Professional management is a huge perk of mutual funds. On top of that, they are diversified, which you will find out in a later section is one of the key elements of successful investing. Mutual funds are also regulated, which means there is a certain amount of fairness and transparency involved when investing in them. Put these great features together with low costs, and you have an extremely powerful investment instrument.

Now, we'll check out a few different types of mutual funds that you should know about.

Index Funds

Index funds are a special kind of mutual fund—one that is *passively managed*. Most mutual funds are constructed from the ground up by the company or portfolio manager that manages them. As we just discussed, you can find all sorts of mutual funds. Some of them focus on Treasury bills, which work like bonds but tend to have very short *maturity rates*, which means you get your payout in a year or so. Other mutual funds might focus on strong diversity, which again is a feature you will learn about later. Index funds in particular are pinned to how certain indexes perform; they replicate the performance of a particular index. This is what we mean by "*passively managed*": index funds piggyback on existing indexes and mimic their growth.

What the hell is an index? I'm glad you asked! An index is a benchmark for a particular asset class that measures how stocks perform for a certain portion of the stock market. We use indexes because there are way too many stocks and shares to keep track of individually. So, we break them into big chunks so we can find out overall how the market is doing. I'm sure you've found yourself flipping through channels late at night and stumbled upon a finance show, where they talk about the "DOW" or the "S&P 500." You probably switched the channel...who wouldn't rather watch the Kardashians, am I right?

Well, the DOW and the S&P 500 are indexes; they're groups that contain information about how certain types of stocks are doing. The

DOW itself (short for the Dow Jones Industrial Average, first dreamed up by Charles Dow over a hundred years ago) tracks the stocks of 30 of the largest and highest-quality companies in the world. You will recognize some of the names right away: Coca-Cola, Apple, Nike, Walmart. If the DOW goes up, that means that confidence in these companies is high and they are getting more valuable, which in turn is seen as an indicator that the economy as a whole is doing well, or at least progressing.

The S&P 500 is short for Standard and Poor's 500. As you may have guessed, it tracks 500 companies (although this number shifts a little bit on occasion). This index is more weighted towards technology and internet companies, and features names like Amazon, Texas Instruments, and eBay.

So, we finally get to index funds, which have been made very popular in recent years by powerhouse firms like Vanguard. Index funds are mutual funds that are tied to different indexes. They invest in companies on a certain index, with the idea being that as those indexes rise, the mutual fund will gain in value and make money for the people participating in it. They aren't limited to just big indexes like the DOW or S&P 500; since an index is basically just a list of companies, anyone can make one. If you really wanted to, you could make an index of, say, streetwear companies like Supreme or Helmut Lang, and try and invest according to your index. I don't recommend doing this, but the idea can be fun! It is important to remember that you can't invest *directly* in an index—the main way to do it for our purposes is through an index fund or an ETF (keep reading!).

TARGET-DATE FUNDS

Target-date funds are a type of mutual fund that targets a specific date to cash out. They are very popular in retirement investing because you can pick a date for retirement, and then let the fund work its magic. Fund managers shake up different parts of the fund depending on how far away the target date is. By design, they are often heavier in stocks earlier in one's career and move to lower risk investments (bonds and money markets) later. One of the great things about target-date funds is that they are thoughtless! They take care of themselves once you have settled on the date that you think you may end your illustrious career—

you are done; they are a point-and-shoot investment tool. But keep in mind that returns are not guaranteed.

ETFS

Extra-terrestrial funds are—oh, sorry, wrong acronym. *Exchange-traded* funds are investment funds that are traded on a stock exchange. They come in many flavors: index ETFs, bond ETFs, stock ETFs, currency ETFs, etc. Many ETFs track an index, so they're not very different from a traditional mutual fund. What differentiates them from mutual funds is that ETFs can be traded quickly, multiple times a day, and change value in real time. ETFs have many of the benefits of mutual funds, and even a few additional ones, like lower fees and transparency.

When you purchase shares in an ETF mapped to an index fund, what you are buying are shares in a separate portfolio (the index fund) that tracks the Nasdaq or DOW or whatever other index you are interested in. Remember how shares work? You are purchasing a "slice of the pie." So while a traditional index fund is going to be valued at the same price throughout the day, ETFs work like stocks in that they fluctuate in value constantly. In addition to this flexibility, ETFs tend to be more tax-efficient than similar investment instruments because you typically only pay taxes on them (as with stocks) when you realize capital gains after cashing out. Tax advantages and flexibility, and as mentioned earlier, lower costs, have made ETFs very popular in recent years, and they are now among the most popular traded securities.

DIVERSIFICATION

This book isn't intended to turn you into a savvy day trader, and there are better resources for learning how to best invest your money in more or less risky instruments. But I do want to impart one very important concept. It's called diversification. This is an important concept, but an easy one to understand and implement.

Ever hear the phrase, "Don't put all your eggs in one basket"? Diversification is the principle that when you spread out your assets and investments in many different directions, you will reap small benefits when they pop up in various ways, but you will also reduce the risk that you will suffer losses when one segment of the economy or asset class drops in value. Take a look at this chart:

2008	2009	2010	2011	2012	2013	2014	2015	2016
Global Bonds 12.00%	Large Cap Growth 37.21%	REITs 27.58%	Bonds 7.84%	REITs 20.14%	Small/Mid Cap 36.80%	REITs 27.15%	Large Cap Growth 5.67%	Small/Mid Cap 17.59%
Bonds 5.24%	Small/Mid Cap 34.39%	Small/Mid Cap 26.71%	REITs 7.28%	International 17.90%	Large Cap Growth 33.48%	Large Cap Value 13.45%	REITs 2.29%	Large Cap Value 17.34%
Cash 1.80%	International 32.46%	Commodities 16.83%	Global Bonds 7.22%	Small/Mid Cap 17.88%	Large Cap Value 32.53%	Large Cap Growth 13.05%	Bonds 0.55%	Commodities 11.77%
Diversified Portfolio -26.72%	REITs 27.45%	Large Cap Growth 16.71%	Large Cap Growth 2.64%	Large Cap Value 17.51%	International 23.29%	Small/Mid Cap 7.07%	Cash 0.03%	REITs 9.28%
Commodities -35.65%	Diversified Portfolio 23.08%	Diversified Portfolio 15.93%	Large Cap Value 0.39%	Large Cap Growth 15.26%	Diversified Portfolio 13.21%	Bonds 5.97%	International -0.39%	Diversified Portfolio 8.73%
Small/Mid Cap -36.79%	Large Cap Value 19.61%	Large Cap Value 15.51%	Diversified Portfolio 0.13%	Diversified Portfolio 11.70%	REITs 3.21%	Diversified Portfolio 5.39%	Global Bonds -2.61%	Large Cap Growth 7.08%
Large Cap Value -36.85%	Commodities 18.91%	International 8.21%	Cash 0.08%	Bonds 4.21%	Cash 0.05%	Global Bonds 0.67%	Small/Mid Cap -2.90%	Bonds 2.65%
REITs -37.34%	Bonds 5.93%	Bonds 6.54%	Small/Mid Cap -2.51%	Global Bonds 1.30%	Bonds -2.02%	Cash 0.03%	Diversified Portfolio -3.20%	Global Bonds 1.57%
Large Cap Growth -38.44%	Global Bonds 1.90%	Global Bonds 6.42%	International -11.73%	Cash 0.07%	Global Bonds -4.50%	International -4.48%	Large Cap Value -3.83%	International 1.51%
International -43.06%	Cash 0.16%	Cash 0.13%	Commodities -13.32%	Commodities -1.06%	Commodities -9.52%	Commodities -17.02%	Commodities -24.66%	Cash 0.27%

Don't worry about all the fancy lingo used. What you are looking at is a list of different types of asset classes over 8 years, and how they performed. Some of them you will recognize from earlier parts of this book, like bonds. If an entry has a positive percentage (like bonds in 2010, 6.54 percent) that means that class of investment did well and increased in value. Those with negative values (looking at you, commodities in 2008) did poorly, and people who invested in them lost money.

The first obvious thing we can learn after looking at this information is that no two years are the same. Some investments do great one year, only to turn around in the next. Some even do badly or well for multiple years in a row. Again, looking at you, 2008! Have you watched *The Big Short* yet? Now's the time! Despite this fluctuation, one thing is clear, and that is that investors who diversified their money into many or all of these categories had the best chance of making money and not losing any. By investing a little bit in each category, you reduce your risk profile. This is an essential technique that investors use to be successful and make the ride much smoother.

COMPOUNDING IS COOL!

I'm talking about compounding! Compounding is so cool that the greatest investors of all time refer to it as "magic." After 20 years in investment and retirement planning, I have found this to be the most important key to building wealth over time. Everyone wants to make lots of money, right? Well, this is one of the answers. Even Einstein was impressed...or was he? As a matter of fact, when I first started writing this book I thought the title would have to do with this, because once you see what happens to numbers over time, it falls under the "you can't make this shit up" category.

A typical textbook definition of compounding might go as follows: compounding is a process where an asset increases its value based on accruing interest. Yes, that's incredibly boring! Let's break down the idea.

When someone borrows money from someone else, the person lending the money typically wants something out of it. No one gives money away for free, after all. So when a bank or some other entity lends someone money, interest can be thought of as the string attached. And yes, credit cards fall under this same category.

If a bank loans someone $100, they expect the money to be paid back in a reasonable amount of time, and they expect to make some money on top of the initial $100. Interest is usually calculated on a monthly basis, so if the bank lends the money at a 2 percent interest rate that means that after the first month, the borrower is on the hook for $102.

It might make sense to assume that after two months, another $2 will be added to the balance, but this is not the case. This is where the compounding element comes in. The next month's interest charge is still 2 percent, but the balance goes up to $104.04 rather than $104.

Where did those 4 cents come from? This is known as interest and is what makes banking work. The interest charge for the second month is calculated based on the existing balance, so 2 percent of the now $102 figure (which is $2.04), not the original $100.

Compounding is a sort of snowball effect. The balance increases based on the previous amount, which is a bit larger because of the interest added from the month before that. The increases are compounded and generate more value all on their own. Interest is the pillar supporting the entire modern banking system. This might seem like a rip-off, a scheme from those sneaky bankers to make money just by letting people borrow it, but the game-changer is this: compound interest works both ways! Instead of being a borrower, let's say you are an investor, and you've got an investment that earns 10 percent a year. You continue to own that fund for 7 years and it continues to do well. Well, now you've benefited from compounding.

YOU ARE #POWERFUL

Yes, you are. In fact, you belong to one of the most powerful consumer generations in history. Your spending habits have the power to kill off entire companies and business models—ones that have been around for decades. Print media is dying, and it's because of you. Big box stores are closing, and it is because you stopped shopping at them. Malls are sending stores packing and are putting in restaurants and gyms, because that is what you badasses want to spend your money on.

When you speak, or open your wallet, companies pay attention. Your opinion, and that of your peers, is one of the most valuable commodities in the world.

Leverage that power. Let your voice be heard. Understand that brands must earn your loyalty. Disappointed in a product? Let them know on Twitter. Get answers and changed policies. As I was writing this section, Star Wars Battlefront II was throwing in the towel and giving in to the demands of consumers. They were calling an end to the ridiculous extra downloadable content that was causing the game to cost thousands of dollars.

Why?

Because when you decide as a group to point your financial assets in a direction (or away from another), that matters.

THE POWER OF GROWTH

Let's do a brief thought experiment. If you have a penny in your bank account today, and that amount doubles every day (so, a 100 percent compound rate), how much would you have after a week? A month? A year? The first one is pretty easy. After two days you would have two pennies. After three days you would have 4 pennies. So after a week, you would have 64 pennies. Not too shabby. After two weeks, you would have 8,192 pennies, or $81.92. Crazy! If I told you what it would be after a month, you wouldn't believe me!

I'm gonna tell you anyway! Pretty soon the math gets out of control. As a matter of fact, after a month you could have over five million dollars ($5,368,709.12, to be precise) and after a year you would have more money than there are atoms in the universe. If this doesn't get across the power of compounding, nothing will! When you are an investor, compounding is a beautiful thing!

A LESSON IN COMPOUNDED GROWTH

A Penny Doubled Every Day for 30 Days

SUN	MON	TUE	WED	THU	FRI	SAT
1 1 Penny	2 2 Pennies	3 4 Pennies	4 $0.08	5 $0.16	6 $0.32	7 $0.64
8 $1.28	9 $2.56	10 $5.12	11 $10.24	12 $20.48	13 $40.96	14 $80.92
15 $163.84	16 $327.68	17 $655.36	18 $1,310.72	19 $2,621.44	20 $5,242.88	21 $10,485.76
22 $20,971.52	23 $41,943.04	24 $83,886.08	25 $167,772.16	26 $335,544.32	27 $671,088.64	28 $1,342,177.28
29 $2,684,354.56	30 $5,368,709.12					

Source: Bloomberg

Albert Einstein needs no introduction and is famous for making stirring statements on a wide variety of topics. He was so influential that he even said things that he didn't say! One saying attributed to the great scientist is:

"Compounded interest is the eighth wonder of the world.
He who understands it, earns it...he who doesn't, pays it."

—Albert Einstein

Whether or not Einstein, in between probing the universe's scientific mysteries, actually said this doesn't really matter. It's true. Compound interest is the driving force behind modern finance, and is the reason that gentleman approached me one a sunny day and thanked me.

Let's say Jack has been working for a few years, but has been spending his paychecks as soon as he gets them and only puts a little bit into a savings account. One day he decides to attend the early-morning enrollment meeting to learn about the company's 401(k) retirement plan. After the advisor makes a very strong case for joining, he decides to join the one with his employer. He is 35 years old and starts off by contributing $1,000. After that, he contributes $100 a month. Over 30 years at this pace, at a 9 percent return rate, he is looking at a value of $184,704 when he turns 62. Of this, $37,000 was directly his money, and $147,704 is the combination of earnings and total return.

Well, this isn't so great. Even with Social Security helping out (more on that later!), he will probably eat through this money in a few years at the most.

IF I COULD TURN BACK TIME

And speaking of eating...one day he is sitting outside his office, munching on some mahi mahi, avocado, and cilantro tacos. He is staring off into space, and even though the tacos are delicious, his retirement prospects are weighing on his mind. He starts to get worried and decides to consult with his friend of many years, David. David is a scientist who has devoted his entire life to the study of time travel. (Hey, bear with me, it's my story!) If he could invent a time machine, surely he should be able to help out with retirement planning.

Well, he arrives at David's lab distraught and fidgety. He explains his situation to David, who listens and nods thoughtfully, then asks him what he would do differently if he had the chance to go back in time. Jack thinks for a minute and says, "You know, I would start investing a few years earlier, and probably contribute a little more each month. I'm sure I would be in a much better situation."

David agrees, and decides to let Jack be the first person to try his experimental time travel technology. This sort of time travel, by the way, reverts the subject back to the age they would be in the year they travel back to. Obviously the story wouldn't work otherwise! Shocked, Jack agrees. He has had a good life, after all. He spent most of his paychecks without planning ahead! If things go wrong, he hasn't lost that much.

So David leads him into the darkest corner of the lab and sits him down in a chair brimming over with wires and dials and buttons. "This is your last chance to back out," David says. Jack looks over to David and says, "Let's do this!"

Suddenly, after a brilliant flash of light, Jack finds himself sitting down at his desk on his first day of the job, 24 years old. The first thing he does is high-tail it to the Human Resources department and sign up for the company's 401(k). This time he starts off his account with every cent he has...just $207.85. But every month from then on out, he contributes $200 a month.

Now, how much do you think he will have by the time he retires, at age 65? He is starting off with a smaller principle, but is going to be contributing for longer, and contributing a bit more each month. Maybe a little more than what he made the first time around? Would you believe me if I told you that by the time he retires, he will have close to **a million dollars** in his 401(k)? Yes, it's amazing actually. This time around, his balance is $856,458, with $96,208 in contributions and **$760,250** in earnings from interest, dividends, and capital appreciation. The first time, his compounding earnings were about four times what he had contributed. **But starting years earlier and contributing a bit more means his compounding earnings were ten times what he contributed.** This is the miracle of compounding, where increasing contributions just a little bit, and giving yourself time, time, and more time will make an earth-shattering difference!

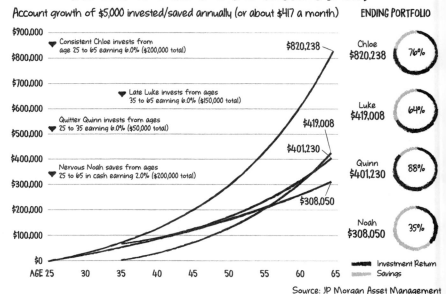

BENEFIT OF SAVING AND INVESTING EARLY

Account growth of $5,000 invested/saved annually (or about $417 a month)   ENDING PORTFOLIO

- Consistent Chloe invests from age 25 to 65 earning 6.0% ($200,000 total) — $820,238 — Chloe $820,238 — 76%
- Late Luke invests from ages 35 to 65 earning 6.0% ($150,000 total) — Luke $419,008 — 64%
- Quitter Quinn invests from ages 25 to 35 earning 6.0% ($50,000 total) — $419,008 / $401,230
- Nervous Noah saves from ages 25 to 65 in cash earning 2.0% ($200,000 total) — Quinn $401,230 — 88%
- $308,050 — Noah $308,050 — 35%

Investment Return
Savings

Source: JP Morgan Asset Management

(IT'S SO EASY!)

As you can see from the chart, Chloe started early and never stopped saving. She also was invested in stocks. Here's the bottom line: **it's crazy *not* to start saving and investing in the market when you are young!**

RULE OF 72

There is a pretty useful trick if you want to experiment with compounding and figure out how quickly your money will grow. There are a lot of calculators online that will help you hash out the details, but try this one first: the rule of 72. This rule will help you determine how long it will take to double your money, assuming a certain rate of return.

Here is how it works: just divide that rate into 72! For example, if you have a 401(k) that is netting an 8 percent return, just divide 72 by 8. The answer is 9…so it will take roughly nine years to double your money at an 8 percent return. This is a good way to do some quick mental math, like if you are trying to impress a friend with your investing prowess.

INFLATION

Ever hear an old-timer say something like, "When I was your age, a hot dog cost a nickel!" Well, that might be a slight exaggeration, but the message behind it is sound; over time, prices have a tendency to increase. We call this "inflation." For commonly-purchased goods like gasoline and food, there is a constant pressure to increase the price. This is because supply might decrease; means of production might become more difficult; demand might increase, etc. When prices go up for these reasons over the span of years, they do not go back down. This is called **cost-push inflation** and is the main culprit behind steadily increasing prices.

I am sure that most of you already have experience with inflation. Maybe you have gotten a "cost of living" raise from your employer to keep up with inflated prices, or you have just noticed how things get a little bit more expensive over time. The annual inflation rate for the United

States is roughly 2 percent as of 2017. What this means is that if you put a dollar in a sock drawer to keep it safe, after a year it can only buy 98 percent of what it used to be able to buy. Why do we need to care about this? **Whenever you are considering investing or saving, you need to beat the rate of inflation to break even.**

Remember the investment dinosaur in chapter one? Well, inflation is part of the reason why the lower-interest accounts discussed earlier in the book are not attractive for long-term investing. After all, what is the point of earning 0.15 percent interest on a dollar if that dollar's worth is going to drop due to inflation? The reason for low-interest savings is still good (use it as a temporary way to save for a rainy day or specific purchasing goal), but in order to make some money, you need to beat inflation to even get out of bed.

Speaking of getting out of bed, let's talk about the inflation of a real-life necessity: coffee. At Starbucks this morning, a tall Caffé Americano costs $2.65. Just a few months ago, it was $2.45. A few years ago, it cost about $2.05. And a little over seven years ago? It was under $2! Now, did the price of coffee go up that much? Not really. So, why did the price of your favorite drink rise over the years? That's inflation in a nutshell, or in this case, a coffee bean. Based on this info, it's safe to assume that same delicious Americano will cost roughly $3.50 for a tall cup in more or less ten years, assuming a 3 percent annual inflation rate.

Why should you care about this? Let's say you put $2,000 in your sock drawer to keep it safe, and inflations increases at the same average of 2 percent a year. After thirty years, the stash will have reduced in value. By that point, $2,000 will only be worth roughly $1,100 in today's money.

SOURCES OF RETURN

Capital Appreciation

"Capital appreciation" is the term we use to describe the increase of the value of an asset based on its market performance. Capital appreciation, interest, and dividends are the engines that drive your retirement plan, and when working together constitute the "total return" of the plan.

There are many factors that can contribute to capital appreciation, and capital appreciation isn't something just stocks and bonds experience. If you buy a piece of property for $100,000, and over time developments in the surrounding area raise the price of all property in that area, that is a type of capital appreciation. This development is often contingent on external factors. When we are talking about investments in stocks, bonds, and mutual funds, external factors can come from all directions. If a company sees research and development pay off in the form of demand for a new product, consumer interest and shareholder confidence can boost that value of that company's stock. Mutual funds in particular focus on maximizing capital appreciation; they cast a wide net when research points towards an increase in the perceived value of different assets.

Dividends

As we discussed earlier, buying stocks is a way to get small bits of ownership in a company. Your shares rise and fall in value as the stock market ebbs and flows, and on a long enough timeline, they are a powerful way to invest in the future. In addition to the paper value of your shares, you can also get paid dividends. Dividends are periodic payouts to shareholders based on the performance of a company. So let's say you bought $500 in stock in a particular company, and then a few months later, the value on your shares has risen to $1,000. Great! You are seeing the power of stock market investing in action. But on top of that, the company also pays out dividends on your shares since they are growing and making a profit. Let's say it's a 4 percent dividend yield, which means that you get paid out 4 percent just for owning so many shares in the company. If you held shares at that $1,000 price for a year, you will have made $40 on top of the increase in value from $500 to $1,000.

Not every company offers dividends. This is particularly true of companies that are younger, and growing quickly. They tend to put their profits into expanding the business and continuing to grow rather than paying out to shareholders.

You may have figured out that a big part of this book is *time*. The longer you have to invest, the better. After all, time is money, whether you are wasting it or saving it! Things become more interesting when you apply this idea to dividends. Historically, dividends have made up a pretty meaningful chunk of the total return of stock market investing. This might not be obvious at first glance, because not all companies offer dividends. In fact, some of the largest and most successful modern tech companies (Google, anyone?) are in this category.

Over time, stocks that pay dividends return *more* than the stock market overall. Dividend-paying stocks have outperformed the overall stock market by around 1 percent. What does this mean? Well, this trend is most significant over decades-long periods, but the point is consistent: dividends are a major contributor of driving total return. As you will discover over the course of this book, anything that powers total return on retirement investing is highly desirable!

Let's wrap up before we finally get to 401(k)s. How do we earn, for example, 8 percent on an investment? We have been talking about three sources of return for any diversified portfolio: capital appreciation, interest income, and dividends. These three sources each have a part to play towards getting you that 8 percent return, and compounding year over year works on *that* figure.

ALL RIGHT! YOU'VE CONVINCED ME! NOW WHAT THE HELL IS A 401(K)?

Now that you are no doubt jumping up and down at how exciting this all is, let's get to the details. A 401(k) is a retirement plan that is generally offered through an employer, which in financial jargon is known as the *sponsor*. It is a retirement account *shell* that allows you to invest money in mutual funds, and sometimes stocks and bonds. When you first decide to sign up for one, you will have to settle on a certain amount of money that you want to put into it. This is called a *contribution*. Your contribution is put into the 401(k) by your employer, who deducts the amount from your paycheck. Usually you pick a percentage amount. The national average for contributions is around 6 percent.

Beginning a 401(k) will take some adjustment when it comes to spending habits, because your paychecks will be a bit smaller. To make this sort of investment more attractive, there is a tax-related perk that comes with contributions. Your employer puts your contribution into the plan *before* taxes are taken out of your paycheck by the government, which means that you will end up with a slightly lower tax liability when everyone's favorite day comes around in mid-April. These are pre-tax contributions. There is also a second tax-related benefit that is much, much more important. This is the fact that 401(k)s are "tax-advantaged," which means that you don't have to pay taxes on the money you earn within your 401(k) until you begin taking money out. We call this tax-deferred growth, and for long-term investments, it makes a *dramatic* difference.

Let's look at a simple example. Suppose you invest $1,000, and you let it sit for 30 years. Your expected annual rate of return is 8 percent, and you are in a pretty normal tax bracket where you are taxed at 28 percent. The future value of your investment if it was taxable is $5,365.91, while the tax-deferred amount would be $10,062.66. Of course, you have to pay taxes on that second figure when you "cash out," but after paying that 28 percent tax rate, you're still left with $7,245.

TAX-DEFERRED VS. TAXABLE ACCOUNTS

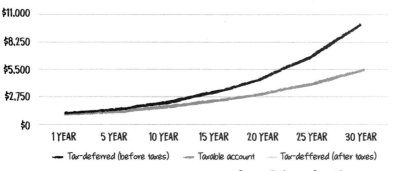

Source: JP Morgan Asset Management

It is possible to withdraw money from a 401(k) early, but it comes with penalties and fees. When cashed out early, a significant portion of the balance is deducted right away (usually in the neighborhood of 20 percent) to cover taxes on the plan's earnings. You can say goodbye to a retirement on Mars in 2050 if you cash out like this. A 401(k) is a powerful tool if you put in the time and money (and the most important ingredient, leaving it alone!), so the consequences of trying to get your fortune early are steep as a deterrent. In short, this is a last resort—don't do it.

THE SLEEP FACTOR

Deciding how much to contribute to a retirement plan can be difficult. You might not *want* to give up some of your paycheck. After all, the latest iPhone will give you much more immediate satisfaction, and you won't reap the rewards of a 401(k) contribution for what, 20, 30 years or more? You might also decide to make a hefty contribution, say 8 percent, and then toss and turn night after night worrying about your (slightly) smaller paychecks, wondering if you should have kept the contribution to 6 percent so that you could have money in case of an emergency, etc.

This is certainly one way to lose sleep. But the main element that goes into the Sleep Factor is the *volatile nature* of the stock market. When investing in stocks, there will always be a degree of uncertainty. Really, it is more than just uncertainty. Volatility can be painful (especially when stocks are going down) and it is the steep price we pay to (maybe) make some money in the future. This is an easy way to lose sleep: worrying deep into the night about how the value of your investments is outside your control at times. Are you the type of person who will freak out after getting a statement showing you lost money? If you get your statement and it's down 10 percent and it absolutely rips your insides apart, then maybe investing in the stock market is not for you.

These two elements (contributions and market uncertainty) play off one another. You control exactly how much you contribute to your investments, but you have almost no control over what the market does with your money, especially in the short term. This relationship means that if you invest 2 percent of your income and lose money, you will still probably sleep better than if you had invested 10 percent. At the same time, if the market goes *up*, you will be much happier if you had invested 10 percent rather than 2 percent. Not to mention, you will have much more money if you defer 10 percent versus 2 percent. It is important to find the proper balance that fits your lifestyle, employment, and goals. Just like in *Fight Club,* "You determine your own level of involvement."

When I go to these meetings and talk with employees about retirement plans, I remind them that there will be down months, quarters, and even years. There is no way to know how to react until it happens. It's not worth losing sleep over the ups and downs of the market, since sleep is much more important than earning higher returns! (Not to mention you have no control over the market, just like the weather.) In advisor-speak we call this "assessing individual risk tolerance," but an easier way to think about it is just as the "Sleep Factor": the sweet spot where you are comfortable with market fluctuations, and not too uncomfortable during those times when the market is making headlines (which almost always means it is going down!) And if you are an insomniac and are awake deep into the night raiding in WoW or binging on Netflix...well, maybe this type of investing is the right amount of badass for you!

Jen remembers her first experience with this quite well. The Asian Currency crisis hit in the third quarter of 2027, and world markets took a dive. Some say it was destined to happen; others claim it was a result of the rhetoric spewed forth by candidates during the presidential election cycle. Jen wasn't worried about *how* it came about. What she cared about was checking her statement one fine morning on her phone and discovering that she was down 15 percent...in just three months!

Most people would panic, losing that much money over what seemed like an overnight period. Like in 2008, the temptation to yank money out of the markets to stop the bleeding was very strong for a number of investors. As the day went on, stocks continued to fall, which meant her retirement fund would be taking a hit as well. Well, Jen didn't panic. After a few breathless moments, she remembered an odd adventure she had had as an undergrad. She remembered seeing a documentary years ago about a gentleman named Warren Buffet and the lessons she had learned from him. Plus, she was still in her twenties and only had $10k in her plan. It's not like she had hundreds of thousands and was retiring in the next few years. So, rather than go with the crowd and pull the emergency brake to get *out* of the market, she calmly decided to stay in the market and actively increase her monthly contributions.

Wait...what? This might seem counterintuitive at first. Why would you buy something when its value is sinking right before your eyes, in real time? If you have something that is losing its worth, why wouldn't you dump it as soon as possible to get some money while you still could? Let's turn to the Oracle himself for some answers.

THE ORACLE SPEAKS

Recently, I stumbled across an article that gave an interesting fact: millennials are under-invested in stocks compared to previous generations. The average millennial is invested in the stock market less than the average 55-year-old. This is crazy!

I'm sure that some of you have heard of Warren Buffett. He's one of the richest people in the world and is famous for being "the most successful investor of all time." The G.O.A.T (AKA the Michael Jordan of investing). He made billions of dollars by investing in the stock market (and he refers to compounding as magic!), and has some insightful things to say about the whole process. I just want to bring a chunk of "wisdom from Warren" to your attention. This is from a shareholder's letter he wrote way back in 1997 (titled, "How we think about market fluctuations"), which makes them basically prehistoric!

A SHORT QUIZ: If you plan to eat hamburgers from In-N-Out throughout your life and are not a cattle producer, should you wish for higher or lower prices for beef? Likewise, if you are going to buy a car from time to time but are not an auto manufacturer, should you prefer higher or lower car prices? These questions, of course, answer themselves.

But now for the final exam: If you expect to be a net saver during the next five or ten years, should you hope for a higher or lower stock market during that period?

Let's think about this for a bit. We know from an earlier section that stocks can be volatile. If the investors are happy and bullish about the future, the value of your stocks, or the stocks in your 401(k), will go up. Hooray! You made money! But if investors are less optimistic about the future, they sell the stocks to get out while they still can make a profit, and your investments lose value. This is a simple example, but you get the point. So in theory, we would want everything to go well, and for all our stocks to go up, right? Not exactly. Let's look at Buffett's answer:

Many investors get this one wrong. Even though they are going to be net buyers of stocks for many years to come, they are elated when stock prices rise and depressed when they fall. In effect, they rejoice because prices have risen for the "hamburgers" they will soon be buying.

This reaction makes no sense. Only those who will be sellers of equities in the near future should be happy at seeing stocks rise. Prospective purchasers should much prefer sinking prices.

This net saver is exactly who you are: someone a long way from retirement. If you are planning on long-term investing and saving money over the course of decades (what Buffett calls in this example a "net-saver"), then for right now you shouldn't worry about low prices: you should welcome them! And thankfully, you will not be disappointed because one of the things you can absolutely count on is that the market will be volatile. There's that word again! It makes me think of a volcano… lying dormant for years before bursting lava sky-high into the air. The market will go up, and it will go down—this is perfectly normal. For the long-term investor, volatility is a friend. Here is the key takeaway:

WITH TWENTY, THIRTY, OR FORTY YEARS ON YOUR SIDE, YOU CAN AFFORD TO TAKE MORE RISK, AND YOU ABSOLUTELY SHOULD!

So don't worry if the markets are doing badly and your 401(k) temporarily goes down for a quarter, or even a year or two. You are in this for long-haul, and rather than be disappointed, don't worry; be happy. This is not easy—money can be emotional, and losing it, even if just on paper, can be quite the downer. Buy more while the buying is good! Not too shabby…you don't often get such solid advice from the distant past! Volatility is a gift from the market to the long-term investor. It's the price we pay for higher returns. And now, Investor Jones will prove it to you!

THE CRISIS OF 2038

It was a gloomy Monday afternoon in the fall of 2038. Jen was working hard but could not keep her eyes off the news. ABC Bank had just fallen victim to the ongoing banking crisis, and since the Dow Jones was down another 3,000 points, or 4 percent, things were looking dire. Folks were more interested in just the return *of* their money, let alone a return *on* their money.

Jen's eyes were drawn to her notification tray, where she had a new entry. She blinked at the notification, and a chat bubble came up on her holographic screen. She was glad that computer manufacturers had come up with this eye implant technology; she always hated using a mouse to get around her computer. The chat invite was from her long-lost friend, Jack.

Jack was upset. Very upset. The crisis was hitting him hard, and he was panicking. Jen did her best to calm him down, especially after he threatened to sell every stock he could find in his retirement plans and go to cash. Or even gold, because he was convinced that **this time is different**. (AKA the four most dangerous words in investing!) Even though every single time one of these events came around, the market has rebounded, he was sure that this time the financial world would end. He even mentioned going into aluminum, of all things.

Jack's fears were not entirely unfounded. After all, the market was down 30 percent over the last three months, and he just couldn't sit and watch his hard-earned funds keep dwindling away almost daily. But he came to Jen for a reason: to ask her advice. Ever since they were in high school, he had respected her, and she always seemed to do the right thing (or at least be one step ahead of almost everybody), especially when it came to money.

Jack: "I'm telling you, this is it. This is the BIG ONE."

Jen: "I'm not going to sell out, Jack."

Jack: "Why on earth not?!"

Jen: "I'm not going to do it. In fact, I am going to increase my contribution like I did 11 years ago when the Asian currency crisis hit. I just got a raise last month, so I am going from 8 percent to 9 percent."

Jack: "WTF...are you crazy?!"

Jen: "I might be! But this just feels like a panic...we have been here before. You know I am a history buff. Throughout history, these things have happened to markets, and the greatest investors of all time never sold out in circumstances like these. Hell, they went shopping for cheap companies whose stock prices had gone down because everyone else sold out of the market."

Jack: "Jen, we are in our mid-thirties. I'm not 22 with $20k to my name. This is real money. I'm finally in six figures, and I can't stand to watch it drop like this—watch it go down to where it was years ago."

Jen tried to talk him out of his plan to cash out. She offered a compromise—leave half or even a third in stocks. Jack said he would think about it. Four days later, the market fell another 6 percent, or 4,000 points. The poor guy broke under the pressure. Not long after market close, Jen received an email from her friend who capitulated that day. It read, "I've sold out." Signed, "Jack."

Jen started questioning herself, wondering if this really was the end. She thought about it more, and then began running through the history in her head. Not going to lie, she was scared as hell! She steeled herself, and continued to believe and stay true to her principles…

INVESTOR JONES AND THE CRYSTAL BALL

How did Jen learn to handle crises like this? Let's go back to her days as a sophomore history major at a small but well-known university. During her time wandering the halls and attending class, she had heard rumors about a certain professor in the business school, known as Investor Jones. He was talked about in hushed whispers…legend had it that he had travelled the world and collected all manner of strange, useful tools in his investing adventures. Foremost of these is the story of how, while on a trip to North Carolina, he came across a crystal ball that would, when asked, reveal the performance of three stocks over a 12-month period.

Jen didn't believe these stories, for the most part, but she was still very curious about Investor Jones and decided to take a trip to his out-of-the-way office to see what he was all about. She wound her way through the halls of the business school until, in a darkened hallway, she saw his name on a door. After knocking, she heard a muffled, "Come in," and opened the door.

On the other side of the small room, there was a man seated behind a desk. He was older and wearing what appeared to be a cowboy hat of some kind. He was perusing some papers on his desk. Jen was a straightforward person, and she dove right into it.

"Professor, my name is Jen, and I am an undeclared major. I'm sorry to barge in on you like this, but I had to ask. What is with these stories about the crystal ball?"

Perhaps it was something in her earnest tone, or maybe Jones was just bored. He looked at her, thought for a moment, stood up, and said, "Follow me."

He turned to his left and opened a door that Jen could have sworn wasn't there just a moment before. She followed him through into another small room. There was a bureau, another desk, and some bookshelves. Everything was covered in dust. He walked over to the bureau, opened the top-most drawer, and gingerly pulled out something small, wrapped in a velvet cloth.

"This might be what all the fuss is about," he said, pulling aside the cloth to reveal a glittering sphere.

Jen caught her breath. *"Are the rumors true?"*

"I won't tell you how it works, but I will tell you what it tells me. The rest you can figure out on your own." With that, he opened yet another door, and she hurried after him.

Jones approached a whiteboard on the near wall and wiped some archaic looking equations off it. He picked up a marker and announced, "This crystal ball tells me how any three stocks will perform over a twelve month period."

"Why twelve months? Why three stocks?"

Investor Jones looked a little flustered and said, "That's not important right now. Do you want to see or not?"

Jen didn't know what to think of this. A key to great wealth, if true. A dotty old professor who was losing his grasp on reality, if false. But still curious, she nodded.

"Let's see it in action," she said.

"Very well," Jones replies. "Name any three stocks."

Jen, a movie buff as well as a budding investor, cleverly responded, "Bluestar, Aerotyne International, and Teldar Paper." Investor Jones nodded thoughtfully and began to stare at the crystal ball.

After a few moments, he seemed to be satisfied. Setting the ball down gently on a filing cabinet, he began writing on the whiteboard. When he stepped aside, Jen saw the following graph:

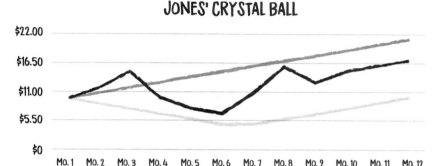

JONES' CRYSTAL BALL

"Now," he said, "you have $1,200 to invest in any of these three stocks. With the knowledge you have acquired about their future performance, which stock would it be best to invest in, if you were to use the entire $1,200 at once, in the first month, to buy shares?"

"That's a no-brainer. Aerotyne performs the best over these twelve months, so you would make the most money putting it all into that stock."

"Very good. Not too hard, but you are right. If you put the entire $1,200 into Aerotyne, you would have more than doubled your money and come out with $2,520. The other two would have ended at $2,040 and $1,200. Now, let's say that instead of buying all at once in the beginning, you invest $100 per month. Which one would be the most successful at the end of the twelve months?"

This was much trickier. Jen thought about it, keeping in mind that buying shares in month five would be advantageous for two of the stocks; the stock would be lower and more cheaply acquired. Unfortunately she wasn't great at mental math. Aerotyne ends at the highest price, but is always a little more expensive to purchase, so she suspects that is a trick answer. She also isn't all that inspired by Teldar Paper, since the value of the stock never gets higher than its initial value, so she guesses Bluestar.

"Wrong!" Jones exclaimed with glee. "If you invested $100 each month in Bluestar, you would have around $1,600 in the end. This is, by

Stocks go up and down every day, and I'm always hearing about people losing their shirt in the stock market. Why bother? During the dot-com bubble that burst, Amazon (yes, they were around back then selling mostly books!) stock went down over 90% during an eighteen-month span. I'll say that again: down 90%! Ouch! But here's the other part of the story: if you invested $1,000 at the IPO price of $18 per share (way, way back in 1997), your investment would be worth more than $634,000 by May 15, 2017. That's twenty years since the company went public. And right about now, I think Jim Cramer would say: BOOYAH!

the way, around what you would get investing $100 a month in Aerotyne. However, if you invested $100 per month in Teldar Paper, you would have closer to $1,700!"

Jones cleared the whiteboard, stashed away his crystal ball, and he and Jen walked back to his main office. He explained to her that the point of this excellent exercise is to show that when an investor is concerned with *long-term returns*, temporary drops in stock value are incredibly beneficial. This is a principle known as "dollar-cost averaging." Over time, investing in a volatile stock will work to your advantage because when the price drops, you can buy more shares. Think about it this way: would you rather have 100 cheap shares worth a mere dollar apiece, or one valuable share worth $80? When prices drop on volatile stocks, you are in a position to snap up those 100 cheaper shares with more overall value. Jones showed Jen one more thing to get across the idea—a simple formula for dollar-cost averaging:

$$\text{average cost per share} = \frac{\text{total amount invested}}{\text{number of shares purchased}}$$

Since $100 can buy more shares when the price is $7 per share rather than when it is $10 per share, the average cost per share for Teldar Paper is lowest. The lower this number, the better the return will be on the investment over twelve months as long as the price goes higher. Magic! (And I promise, no more equations!)

We will head back to reality now, and leave Jones and Jen for another time. This brilliant story illustrates what Buffett was saying in his puzzle. Investors should welcome drops in prices if their goal is to be net savers. This should boost the confidence of everyone who is getting involved with a retirement plan like a 401(k). There is no need to get overly worried if the market tanks. Actually, I will assume that over your lifetime, the market will go down, sometimes hard and fast. If during these times you can be bold and feel comfortable during the slump, then once the market rights itself, you will have made even more than if things just kept slowly going up!

POP QUIZ!

Okay, I'm not really giving you a pop quiz. But remember when I told you to remember a few key phrases? Let's revisit them now to illustrate some of these points before going on to different kinds of retirement plans. In case you forgot, the terms I wanted you to remember were **S&P 500** and **net-saving**.

Now, let's rewind the clock to 1998. Everything is peachy. Destiny's Child is still together. The internet is growing and has changed the way we live our lives. Tech companies are booming, as more and more innovators start companies to make the most of these technological tools. The economy is strong. And then, a few years later, it all came crashing down...and Y2K wasn't the culprit!

In the years leading up to 2000, tech savvy people weren't the only ones making themselves busy. Investors were eager to put money into these companies, and they had built one hell of a bubble. A *bubble* is a complicated thing, but I'll describe it to you in an easy way. Let's say you have a fruit tree in your backyard. You wake up one morning to a shocking sight: your tree is growing not only apples, but oranges and bananas as well! Amazing! Well, being the clever money-maker that you are, you decide to put this tree to good use. You go door to door, taking orders for apples, oranges, and bananas, and undercut the price of these fruits at the local supermarket. Everyone loves that they can get their fruit right down the street for cheap, and you get a ton of orders.

It becomes clear that you will have a hard time filling all the orders by yourself, so you start hiring friends to come help you pick the fruit. They expect to be paid, so you need to increase your output. At the same time, availability of the fruits drops at the grocery store. Suddenly, you are the only one offering fruit. Things are getting exciting!

Well, one day some investors come to your door. They are interested in purchases shares of your little company. You agree, and make some money. The investors then sell and buy those shares on the stock market. People are aware of the shortage at other places of apples, oranges, and bananas, so you get more business. Pretty soon, your fruit, company, and shares in your company are worth an insane amount of money. Shares and products are selling for way more than they are probably actually worth, but everyone is caught up in this new business model and gets ahead of themselves.

You have created a bubble. In simple terms, a bubble occurs when asset prices go through the roof, but the market can't reasonably maintain those prices because they aren't actually worth that much. In our example, this is demonstrated by the fact that a shortage in fruit at other places is just temporary. This trend can only go on for so long, after all. Just like a soap bubble grows and grows until it suddenly **pops**, so too do market bubbles grow and grow until *they* pop.

Well, one day fruit comes back to the grocery store. A lot of fruit. The grocery store prices go back under yours, and your company loses value. Stock in your company that was bought for $100 yesterday is suddenly only worth $4 today. People who invested in your company lose a ton of money, and with these dropping prices, the stock market contracts overall. Your bubble has burst.

So back in the late 1990s, investors had created a tech bubble, also called the "dot-com bubble." They had pumped up the value of stocks in new internet and tech companies way beyond what they could reasonably be worth, and it was only a matter of time before that bubble burst. It did, finally, from 2000 to 2002. There were just too many tech and internet companies competing in the same fields, worth too much money, for the bubble to continue. Many companies went out of business completely, and some of those went out with some crazy scandals. The stock market took a huge hit, including the S&P 500. Many investors pulled their money from this and other indexes, and they plummeted in value.

Let's move forward a few more years, into the mid-to-late 2000s. Things had *finally* gotten better. The stock market had recovered, and in July 2007, the S&P 500 had closed at its highest point in history: over 1,500. That same month, the DOW closed at *its* highest point in history: over 14,000. What most people didn't realize at the time, however, was that we were in the middle of *another* bubble—the housing market bubble. This bubble was very, very complicated, but thankfully there is a fantastic movie that describes what happened: *The Big Short.* This is a must-see if you want to understand how bubbles work and why our economy is the way it is today.

The housing bubble, in a nutshell, was defined by the ever-increasing value of houses and the constant availability of debt (and the *misuse* of debt, or leverage...but that's another story). Housing prices just kept going up and up and up because more and more people were buying houses. It was an unprecedented period of growth, but it was backed by very bad mortgage practices. Basically, lenders were giving mortgages to anyone, regardless of their credit score. You could get a loan to buy a house no matter what. Eventually, people who should never have been given these mortgages, because they couldn't pay them off, just stopped making payments. From 2006 to 2008, dozens of banks and mortgage lenders either filed for bankruptcy or failed completely.

This bubble began bursting in 2007, when the failures of these institutions caught up with the stock market. On September 29th, 2008, the DOW dropped a whopping 777.68 points. By March 2009, it was sitting at 6,594.44. It had lost over *half* of its value. In October 2008, the S&P 500 had dwindled to 968.80, a fraction of its worth from a year before. 401(k) plans were decimated, the New York Stock Exchange was closed multiple times to stop the bleeding, and people began talking about government bailouts. It was one of the most catastrophic economic and market collapses in history. Many people lost a ton of money.

Why am I telling you all this? This sucks! It was terrible! Why this long, sad story? Well, from 1998 to the present day, we can see a crystal clear example of the principles of net-saving in action. Let's say you invested in S&P 500 companies quite a bit in 1998. You see some gains, and then in 2001 everything goes down the toilet when the dot-com bubble bursts. As things get FUBAR and the value of stocks drop across the board, you have three options: sell now and cut your losses, stay the course and leave your investments alone, or buy even more when the prices drop. If you had sold your stocks while you still had a chance to stem the bleeding, you may have only lost a little bit of money, or if you were SUPER lucky, you may have ended up a little bit ahead or where you were to begin with. If you stayed the course, you lost money. And if you bought even more, you lost a TON of money.

But let's jump forward in time again (getting dizzy yet?) to 2005. If you had gone with the first option, selling, then you wouldn't be that far along in your investment career. Being conservative in your investments means you were out of the market for the up and down days, which means you missed some big gains that occurred as the S&P recovered from its lows during the aftermath of the bubble burst. If you had stayed the course, well, look at that! You made money! You may have been in the red for over 5 years, but sure enough, the market recovered and you were invested when the market saw big gains. Congratulations!

If you had gone with the third option, digging in deep and investing even more, you saw the biggest gains of all. You took a risk and bought stocks when they were very low, and your existing stocks dropped in value. There were some lean, scary years for sure. But it all paid off, and in 2005 your investments would have netted you a ton of money. Sound familiar? What I am describing is exactly what Jen saw when she visited Investor Jones, only instead of seeing the trend in a single stock over a few months, I am describing it in terms of the *entire* market over the course of years. The same principles apply.

Now, as we saw with the housing bubble crash, the same thing happened all over again a few years later. In fact, it was even worse. Way worse. But everything works out the same! If you panicked and sold stock in 2008 as the markets were tanking, you most likely lost money. If you stayed put and didn't mess around with your investments, then ten years later in the present day, you are looking at gains, since you made the most of being in play during the big jumps. And if you invested even more—well, like before, you can guess what happens.

You will have noticed that a key factor in all of this is *being invested on the right days*. There is no way to predict when the market will see a huge jump. No matter what people may promise you, there is no way to tell what these days are going to be. For example, no one would have been able to magically predict that on March 23rd, 2011, the S&P 500 would have seen one of its biggest point gains in history. If you were invested on that day, good for you! You made a crapload of money! If you weren't, because you had withdrawn your money a few months before when we were smack dab in the middle of one of the biggest market contractions in history, too bad. You missed out. And if you had, a few months earlier, bought even more stock when prices were crazy low, then you made the smartest move of all.

So let's tie this together with those two terms: **S&P 500** and **net-saving**. We are going to cover a 20-year period at first, from 1993 to 2013, to see us through the creation, busting, and recovery from the two big bubbles. Now, if you had invested $10,000 in the S&P 500 in 1993 and stayed invested for the entire time, then in 2013 your investments would be worth $58,332. This is a pretty whopping gain, and indicates a 9 percent return or so. If you had gotten spooked during the bubble periods, gotten out of the market, and missed the *10 best days* of investing during those volatile periods, you would have a little over $29,000, a modest 5.49 percent gain. Okay, you still made money, but the difference is pretty staggering. Missed the best 30 days? You made less than a single percent in return, or $11,984. How about missing the best 60 days? Well, in that case you actually lost money, and your investments would be worth less than $5,000.

Now let's look at the *really* crazy numbers. Let's go back to 1976. Guess what your initial $10,000 would get you if you had stayed the course through to 2016? I'm pretty sure none of you would have come close to the answer...**$641,305**. Blows your mind, right? That's a 10.9 percent return! Now, let's say we *slightly* bump that return rate up to 11.8 percent. That tiny little 0.9 percent increase was worth an extra $239,648. Now let's say you had picked a mutual fund for that period of time, which netted you 13 percent. Grand total? **$1,399,747**! (And because I'm sure you're asking, *yes*, this is real.)

> Wait a minute, did I read that right? The difference between earning 10.9 percent a year and 13 percent a year (a 2.1 percent difference) is more than *double* your money over a 40-year period?

So, if you have the goal of being a net-saver (and you 1,000 percent should!), the answer is obvious: once invested, don't get out of the market if something happens and the stock market drops. The risk that you will miss the best days and lose money overall is just too high, especially since historically the biggest daily gains happened after really down days. Stick with it! The market goes up

and down all the time, and the lesson here is that no drop is permanent. You are young, and have all the time in the world to let the market correct itself and keep earning you money. Just let history be your guide. (And on top of all that, we have another handy little lesson built into this example: a single percentage point is all that separates a $600,000 Bugatti from a $1.4 million Laundalet on a long enough timeline!)[1]

I WANT TO PLAY A GAME #PAYTOPLAY #PAYTOWIN

No saws here. I wouldn't do that to you, not unless you have some cryptocurrency tip I don't.

Think of investing as the ultimate game. You won't see teenagers on ESPN strapped to gaming PCs, maxing their APM investing in derivatives at lightning speed. We have machines for that. (Seriously, look up quantitative investing, it's cool stuff!)

There is no investing world championship either. But investing is a still a game. It is a competition. It is a system, with rules and refs and constantly changing variables and human error. There is no room to make mistakes, especially when you are young. You need to be on top of your game. And like most endeavors in life, they don't hand out trophies for just showing up and being on a team!

---

1   Note: As much as he would like to, the author does not condone the purchase of million-dollar cars…yet.

You've got shit to do. We have self-driving cars and AI in our living rooms. The future is here, and things are just going to get faster. Why waste time doing things the old way—the way your parents did? You are learning and making up the rules of the game at the same time. It is time to win.

You want to win? Don't compromise. Be ruthless when you have to be. Give up things now (maybe even other games); give up temporary, unnecessary comforts if you have to, in exchange for a better strategic position down the line. You carry the key around in your pocket, so don't stay strapped to a radiator in a torture basement. Metaphorically speaking.

No more excuses. Go out there and get what's yours.

BACK TO THE FUTURE!

Now that I have hammered the principle of net-saving into your head, and with the basics of a 401(k) under our belt, let's return to them and talk about some of the other features you might come across. One of the golden tickets when it comes to employer-offered 401(k) s is matching contributions. If your employer offers this, take it! Take it yesterday! In a matching contribution plan, for every dollar you put in, your employer will put in a matching amount. This can effectively double the value of your contributions, and it drastically increases the speed with which your plan will rocket you to Filthy-Rich Town. Remember Jack in our time-traveling example? If his employer matched his contributions, he would retire with over $1.5 million in his 401(k). That's just crazy! Just like your tax benefits, employers get nice tax perks for contributing matching amounts to their employee's plans. On top of that, employers love to offer these plans as they tend to attract top talent in the field, and then retain good employees when they get them locked in. In theory, everyone wins!

Think about it this way: if your employer matches your contributions, you are getting **FREE MONEY**. If you contribute $100 a month to your 401(k) and your employer matches it, you have made $100 each month for absolutely nothing. So far we have talked about different returns—numbers like 3 or 7 or 9 percent. Well, employer-matched contributions to a 401(k) are a stunning 100 percent return—up to the contribution limit, of course. Can you imagine if the bank down the street from your house put up a sign one day saying, "For each $1,000 you put into an account with us, we will *give you* $1,000"? The line to make deposits would probably run around the block. Probably out of the city, to be honest. Every single person who knew about it would sign up. Well, employer-matched contributions are doing just that!

> Max out your contributions up to your employer's contribution level. If your employer has a matching limit, then you should absolutely hit it. There is really nothing to compare to a risk-free, 100 percent return on investment.

VESTING

There is one very important wrinkle to keep in mind if your employer offers any contributions to your 401(k). Employers who contribute to employees' 401(k)s want to keep those employees as long as they can. That is the whole point of offering such a plan, as mentioned: attracting and retaining skilled staff. In order for this to work out for employers, certain restrictions are placed on how flexible you can be with your 401(k).

Always remember that any money you contribute to your 401(k) is yours. You don't have to worry about it being taken away if you decide to change jobs and take your 401(k) with you. However, if you decide to do this with a 401(k) that your employer has contributed to, you might not be able to take all the money. Money contributed by your employer vests over time, which means it becomes "yours" at a certain rate, year after year. As money vests, it becomes yours, and you can take it with you even if you leave your job. The rate at which the money vests varies from plan to plan. Some plans vest at whatever percentage rate would make you fully vested at five years of employment, while others might be at a specific percentage, like 33 percent per year. Still others might not vest at all until a certain number of years have passed; then, the money becomes yours all at once. However your plan works, learn the vesting schedule.

Here is an example of a common vesting schedule referred to as 2/20 vesting, just so you have a visual to see how it works.

YEARS OF SERVICE	% VESTED
2 years	20%
3 years	40%
4 years	60%
5 years	80%
6 years	100%

WHAT'S THE CATCH?

So nothing this badass can be totally free. In addition to vesting conditions, there are a number of other restrictions you might come across when looking at your 401(k) options.

Unfortunately, many employers don't allow you to contribute to your 401(k) until after you have been employed for a certain amount of time (usually this is three months or a year). You essentially have to prove yourself to your employer, and only *then* can you contribute to your plan. Remember how *huge* of a difference a little bit of extra time can make when investing for retirement? Well, it doesn't make sense to lose that year. If you start a job that you like, but the 401(k) has this restriction, go ahead and sign up for it, but *also* get a Roth IRA or traditional IRA (more on those in a minute). During that year where you can't contribute to the 401(k), contribute to the IRA instead. It is perfectly fine to have both!

Like most things, 401(k) plans have fees. You need to very carefully read your 401(k) plan documentation (in the finance world, these are known as "SPDs": summary plan descriptions) to see if fees are covered by your employer or not. These fees can come in many forms—investment fees, plan management and administration fees, and more. The key thing to remember is that any reduction in your 401(k) plan's value drastically reduces its power to *compound* in your favor. The US Department of Labor released an information pamphlet a few years ago about these fees, and it addresses the impact fees can have on your retirement:

Assume that you are an employee with thirty-five years until retirement and a current 401(k) account balance of $25,000. If returns on investments in your account over the next thirty-five years average 7 percent and fees and expenses reduce your average returns by 0.5 percent, your account balance will grow to $227,000 at retirement, even if there are no further contributions to your account. If fees and expenses are 1.5 percent, however, your account balance will grow to only $163,000. The 1 percent difference in fees and expenses would reduce your account balance at retirement by 28 percent.

That is huge! It might not seem like small fees hurt all that much, but when we are talking about years and years of accumulated fees eating into that sweet, sweet compounding, the results can be staggering.

YOU LIKE ROLLERCOASTERS...RIGHT?

Historically, 401(k) values will go up and down like the stock market if your 401(k) is primarily invested in stocks. During the financial crisis of 2008 brought on by the collapse of the sub-prime mortgage and derivatives scheme (I would rather be stung by a thousand hornets than torture you by describing this nonsense!) many people lost quite a bit of the value in their 401(k)s. The thing to keep in mind is that these losses were temporary. If you did nothing and kept contributing at the same rate, that meant you were buying back at a good price during low periods. It was a long, difficult path to recovery, but the damage done is largely gone. My advice? If aliens invade and Wall Street loses it and the stock market plummets, don't panic. The temptation to freak out and either stop contributing or even cash out with what little you have left in your plan is always a bad decision. Just hole up, turn on some Netflix, and be patient. Remember, when it comes to retirement investing in a 401(k), having time is a beautiful thing!

Remember, every market downturn in history has ended in an upturn. Stay calm and KOI—Keep On Investing!

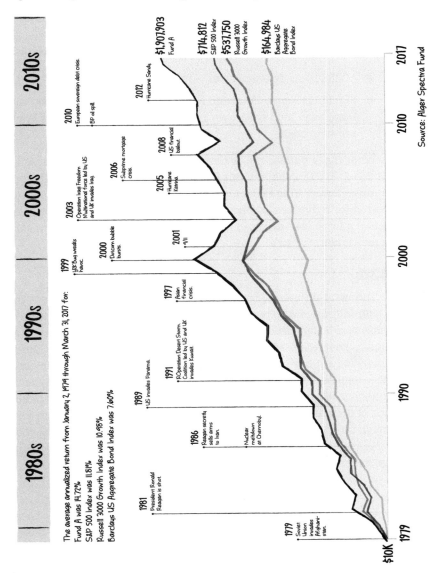

The average annualized return from January 2, 1979 through March 31, 2017 for:
Fund A was 14.72%
S&P 500 Index was 11.81%
Russell 3000 Growth Index was 10.48%
Barclays US Aggregate Bond Index was 7.60%

1979 Soviet Union invades Afghanistan.

1981 President Ronald Reagan is shot.

1986 Reagan secretly sells arms to Iran.

Nuclear meltdown at Chernobyl.

1989 US invades Panama.

1991 Operation Desert Storm. Coalition led by US and UK invades Kuwait.

1997 Asian financial crisis.

1999 Y2K bug wreaks havoc.

2000 Dotcom bubble bursts.

2001 9/11

2003 Operation Iraqi Freedom. Multinational force led by US and UK invades Iraq.

2005 Hurricane Katrina.

2006 Subprime mortgage crisis.

2008 US financial bailout.

2010 European sovereign debt crisis.

BP oil spill.

2012 Hurricane Sandy.

$1,907,903 Fund A

$714,812 S&P 500 Index

$531,750 Russell 3000 Growth Index

$164,984 Barclays US Aggregate Bond Index

$10K

1979 1980s 1990s 2000s 2010s 1990 2000 2010 2017

Source: Alger Spectra Fund

BUT MY EMPLOYER DOESN'T OFFER A 401(K)!

Many of you won't be in a position to invest in a 401(k). Our lives take us in many directions—perhaps even to a company that doesn't offer a retirement plan. Thankfully, there are retirement options available for everything short of art theft and bond forgery. In this section, we will go over some of these other retirement plans and discuss the pros and cons of each.

The main alternatives to a 401(k) that you should be aware of are:

- 403(b) plans, for employees of non-profits and other institutions.

- SEP IRAs, Simple IRAs, and Roth IRAs, most commonly used by those who own their own business or are in some other way self-employed.

What these various plans have in common that they share with traditional 401(k) plans, and this is very much in your favor, is that they are tax-deferred. This means you reap the benefits of having money invested for retirement before taxes, allowing you to actually not take much of a hit to your expected income if you budget correctly and make the proper contributions.

403(b)

The main difference between a 401(k) and a 403(b) has less to do with individual employment and more to do with the organizations themselves. Many hospitals, schools, and non-profits have a special tax status to keep them afloat in an otherwise cutthroat economy. These employers must have a 501(c)(3) tax-exempt status to offer these plans. Rather than dust off some archaic IRS documentation in order to explain, let me just tell you simply that because these organizations receive much of their funding either directly from the government, or indirectly through tax breaks, there are special restrictions on how they can spend their money. This manifests itself in many ways, including how they can offer retirement plans to employees.

When it comes to the nitty-gritty details, 403(b) plans work the same way as 401(k) plans. An outside administrator manages the account, and employees contribute. Both plan types have the same limit to yearly contributions, which as of the writing of this book is $18,000 for those under age fifty. If you are making enough money to contribute this much each year to your 401(k) or 403(b), congratulations...you are well ahead of the curve!

One major difference between these plans is that funds become available earlier in most 403(b)s, which can be a way to get your cash at a younger age and avoid the penalties associated with early 401(k) withdrawal. The trade-off is that, unlike many 401(k)s, employers who offer 403(b)s typically don't match contributions as much. There is a lot of flexibility involved with both plans, and the most pertinent details are best gotten from your employer. The point is not to worry if you don't have access to a traditional 401(k); there are other options.

IRAs (OR, I AM GETTING SICK OF THESE ABBREVIATIONS!)

IRA stands for "individual retirement account" and is the option most used by those who run their own small business or are self-employed. There is no middle-man, since the individual works directly with the managing firm on the account. Remember earlier, when I mentioned that the employer generally picks a plan from among several options, then offers it to the employee? Well, since there is no company in charge of this task, it is up to the individual to handpick the different investment options within the IRA plan (remember, these are usually stocks, bonds, ETFs, and mutual funds). As a result, there are very few restrictions on the investment tools within the IRA. So, if you are extra clever, have a background in finance, or figured out time travel without telling the rest of us, an IRA can have more earning potential, provided you went with well-performing investments.

There is one major drawback to IRAs: the contribution limit is much lower. Currently, there is a yearly contribution cap of $5,500 for you young folks, and $6,500 for those over 50. You can feed a traditional IRA much less than you can feed a 401(k) or 403(b), which tends to balance out with the investment flexibility. Much like those other plans, however, money is fed to the IRA before taxes, so you still get that perk.

Roth IRAs, Simple IRAs, SEP IRAs, YOLO, and the NFL

No, there isn't a retirement plan with an "NFL" abbreviation. The first three are real though, and round out this brief overview of individual retirement accounts. I'm sure you don't want the excitement to end, but don't worry, there will be plenty of financial poetry to come!

I have mentioned many times that one of the big benefits of these plans so far is that the contributions are made before taxes, so you save a little bit on your investments. This is where a Roth IRA (named after Senator William Roth, if you were wondering) differs. In this type of plan, contributions are made after taxes. So, you get your paycheck, the government steals some, and you are left with your take-home pay. After all that, contributions can be made to a Roth IRA. Losing the pre-tax benefit of traditional plans is made up for the fact that when you withdraw money from the fund in order to pay for retirement, the withdrawals are tax-free. In short, you give up a present advantage in exchange for a later one.

SEP IRAs are plans geared towards smaller companies, sole proprietors, independent contractors, and freelance workers. Usually the plan is managed by the small business owner or individual, and tax deductions apply to any contributions made. Contributions to a SEP IRA are tax deductible, so you can lower your tax liability based on your contributions and save when tax time comes. Like with traditional IRAs, no taxes need to be paid until withdrawal. SEP stands for "Simplified Employee Pension" and they are just a little bit easier and cheaper to administer. There are some restrictions on them that might not make them attractive to employees who have access to something like a 401(k), but there is one *big* advantage that should be mentioned. The contribution limit for SEP IRAs is much higher than the other plans we have talked about, and as of this writing employees can contribute up to 25 percent of their pay or $54,000 a year to their plan, whichever is lower.

The following chart will serve as a handy reference for all of the details we have just gone over.

	401(K) AND 403(B)	ROTH IRA	TRADITIONAL IRA	SEP IRA
ANNUAL CONTRIBUTION LIMIT	$18,000 for those under age 50	$5,500 if you are under age 50	$5,500 if you are under age 50	25 percent of your income, up to $54,000
AGE REQUIRED TO AVOID PENALTIES FOR WITHDRAWAL	59.5 years	59.5 years	59.5 years	59.5 years
TAXES FOR WITHDRAWALS	Taxed as income	Tax-free	Taxed as income	Taxed as income
TAXES FOR CONTRIBUTIONS	Pre-tax income	After-tax income	Pre-tax income	Pre-tax income

I GOT NINETY-NINE PROBLEMS, BUT MY FIVE RETIREMENT ACCOUNTS AIN'T ONE...

Now that you are familiar with the different types of retirement accounts, you are ready to learn about having more than one. There are several reasons why you might want to have more than one plan. The benefit you get from starting your retirement plan early on in your professional life should be clear by now. But what if you get off to a late start?

Let's revisit one of the baddest girls in school, Jen. After her enlightening meeting with Investor Jones, she was bubbling over with excitement. The investing confidence she gained after Jones' crystal ball lesson put a skip in her step, and she bounded back to her dorm room to explore further.

Her roommate, Katie, was deeply entrenched in study. She was a biomedical engineering major, a very straight-laced type, and a straight-A student. She always had her nose in a book—something long, technical, and boring. Usually, when Katie was so focused, Jen would never bother her.

But today, she just *had* to talk to someone. She had seen the future! She understood the secrets of net-saving! Who wouldn't want to hear about it? Well, apparently, Katie. After placing her finger on the page and greeting her roommate, Katie's eyes glazed over once Jen started going off about fluctuations in the market, the Sleep Factor, and more.

"Jen, I get that this is interesting to you, but I just can't get excited about it," Katie said. "How could I get excited about this kind of thing when I have so much to study on much more interesting topics? After all, retirement is so far away…I'll think about it later."

"One day you will wish you had paid attention!" Jen responded, realizing that she was suddenly very hungry.

The conversation ended there, and they never really picked it back up. The two scurried off to dinner at the student cafeteria, and they went on with their lives a few years later. After graduating, Katie landed a great job at an engineering firm. She made all the right moves, worked hard, and began to accomplish interesting things in her field. However, she never really thought twice about saving, 401(k)s, compounding, or anything else that Jen had told her about all those years before. And speaking of Jen, she joined the Peace Corps, traveled the world for years, had a number of odd jobs, and had a ton of incredible experiences.

She had an amazing time, as you might expect. She saw a wide array of cultures, met fascinating people, and picked up a second language while working under the table at a fancy restaurant in Madrid. After a few years, she found her way back to the US and got a job as a translator and paralegal at a law firm. In all of her adventures, she had been careful to stick to some of the key principles she had learned about over the years. She kept them all in mind, and no matter where she was and what she was doing, she was making the maximum contributions to her retirement investments and saving when she could.

Katie worked happily at the engineering firm for a while, but never paid attention to Human Resources bulletins about the firm's retirement plan. Then one day she saw an update on Facebook from Jen, saying something about being on track to retire early, along with a link to a

Wall Street Journal article. Memories from college came back to her. She remembered that day when Jen had come into their dorm room bursting with excitement about arcane topics like mutual funds and something about a crystal ball. She realized suddenly that she may have lost a lot of time, and that she probably should have paid closer attention! She was thirty-three years old, and although she made a good salary, she spent her money freely. She had no savings and no retirement fund, which meant she had no way, when the time came, to retire comfortably. She was not dead…but definitely behind the eight ball.

This bummed her out, so she texted Jen. They met for lunch, and Katie expressed her dilemma. She didn't want to be stuck working forever! What could she do?

Jen may have been bouncing around the globe doing fun things, and she wasn't an expert in finance by any stretch of the imagination, but she had stuck to a few enduring principles—the very basic and simple ones that she had picked up over the years and which you have been reading about. The Rule of 72. The 10 to 40 percent rule. Holding the course with an eye on net-saving. So even though she wasn't a financial wizard, she had gotten in on the 401(k) early, and had saved all she could. When they met up for coffee that day, she was miles ahead of Katie when it came to realizing her dreams down the road…whatever they may be.

Jen gave her a crash course in the topics you've just read about, and assured her that it wasn't too late to start planning for retirement. Katie was making a decent salary, $65,000 a year, and had no debt. This meant that she had many options, if she could cut back on her spending. Jen told her about 401(k)s and IRAs and helped her friend formulate a plan.

In this book we have talked about how there are contribution limits to 401(k)s. What if you end up in a situation like Katie's, where you have to play catch up in order to retire successfully? You are behind the curve already, and only being able to contribute $18,000 a year to a 401(k) means there is a limit to how much you can try to regain lost ground. Luckily, there is no reason you can't have multiple retirement accounts and overcome the contribution limits of one by contributing to others.

There are some quirks, like income limits, that come with juggling multiple retirement accounts, but in general, there are no problems with pairing a 401(k) with an individual IRA of some kind, either Roth or traditional. Someone like Katie could contribute $18,000 a year to her employer's 401(k), and then put another $5,500 towards a Roth IRA in order to make the most of her income. Having a 401(k) doesn't put any restrictions on your ability to also have an IRA. However, Katie couldn't contribute the maximum $5,500 to both a traditional IRA *and* a Roth IRA, since the laws governing IRA contributions take them all together rather than individually.

KEEP ROLLIN' ROLLIN' ROLLIN'...

If you do leave a job where you had a 401(k), keeping that account open isn't your only option. If you are worried about having to keep track of multiple 401(k)s and would prefer to keep your retirement funds localized, you can do different things with the old account. In addition to leaving the 401(k) as-is (a totally fine option in most cases) and withdrawing it as a lump sum (a bad idea), you can also "roll over" the account into the new employer's 401(k) plan or, because it's taxable if you take it early, roll over the account into an individual plan like an IRA.

I say leaving the 401(k) is fine in most cases because some 401(k) plans have a special rule where if the 401(k) value is under a certain amount (as of this writing, $5,000), the employer can close the account and give you money. This adds an unnecessary complication. Since you have already invested the money into a plan, having to reinvest it will slow you down, since you probably won't be able to put it all into a new plan right away. If your old 401(k) plan has this feature, it is better to roll over the account or transfer it. The other problem is that if you leave a job but keep the 401(k) open, you can't make any more contributions to it. You will still get the benefits of compounding, but you won't be able to speed the process up by contributing more. If your old 401(k) is above the close-out amount and you are okay with letting it sit at your now "previous employer's" retirement plan and compound over time, it is safe to leave it alone—again, as long as it is over the limit.

Rolling over a 401(k) into an IRA is a pretty straightforward process. What happens is your money is transferred over to an IRA, and since both IRAs and 401(k)s are tax-advantaged, you keep all the same benefits. You also avoid the early-withdrawal penalties, since you technically aren't cashing out. You will end up paying fees to the company that manages the rollover and the IRA, however. There are some advantages to rolling over a 401(k) into an IRA, the primary one being more control over and options for the investments within the plan. Remember, employers generally pick the investment options within the 401(k) they offer their employees; even if you are a clever investor like Jen, you are stuck with the "investment menu" that the employer picked out. However, most people aren't interested in trying to micromanage their investments, so the "more control" perk might not be very important to you.

For many people who leave one job for a new one, there is also the option to roll over the old 401(k) into a new 401(k). It may be cheaper in the end, and is definitely the simplest choice. For many people, simpler is better. I would recommend rolling over a 401(k) into an IRA if some of these factors are in play:

- You are like Jen, and you understand managing an investment account and want full control over it, and may even want to buy stocks in your IRA.

- You don't get a new job right away and don't have access to a new 401(k) plan but want to keep contributing to a retirement plan.

- Your old 401(k) is under the close-out amount and you are looking at turning invested money into un-invested money, setting you back on your path to retirement.

- The old 401(k) plan is poorly managed, and your previous employer picked par or subpar investment choices.

The last option is transferring the money in the old 401(k) into a qualified annuity. A qualified annuity is a type of account that accepts contributions on a pre-tax basis just like a 401(k), and slowly grows over time. Qualified annuities are one of the more complicated products in the entire financial world, and this last section is meant just to introduce the idea to you. There are *many* types of qualified annuities, and to really dig into them, check out the "Further Reading" section at the end of this book.

So now that we have gone over options for your old 401(k), let's recap the important bits. If you have left a job, and have an old 401(k), consult this overwhelming flow chart on the following page:

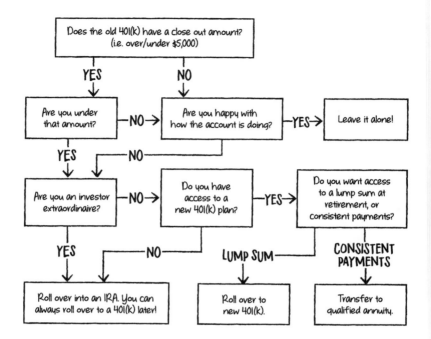

PENSIONS

If you have never heard of a pensions outside of the occasional movie reference, you are not alone. Pension plans used to be everywhere, but they are slowly going the way of the dinosaur:

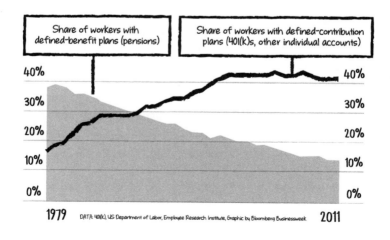

Share of workers with defined-benefit plans (pensions)

Share of workers with defined-contribution plans (401(k)s, other individual accounts)

1979   DATA: 401(k), US Department of Labor, Employee Research Institute, Graphic by Bloomberg Businessweek   2011

As you can see, 401(k)s (defined contribution plans) have gotten much more popular, and pensions have dwindled. This is for many reasons, most of which are bogged down by complicated history we won't get into.

Anyway, we are mainly going to be talking about *defined benefit pensions*. In a nutshell, this type of pension is a contractual agreement between an employee and an employer where the employee agrees to work for a company for a certain amount of time while making contributions to the plan, and the employer agrees to pay the worker a certain amount of money each year after retirement, forever. Usually the payout depends on two factors: "tenure," or the amount of time worked, and salary. The longer you stay at a company and the higher your salary, the larger your pension payouts will be.

Not all pension plans work the same way, but most of them require the employee to contribute a certain amount of their salary to the pension fund, so in that sense they work like a 401(k). The main difference is that you don't see any of the investing features of the pension plan; your employer is responsible for the management of the fund, and is in charge of any investment decisions once you make your contributions. What do modern pension plans look like, where can you find them, and are they worth it?

Who Still Offers Pensions?

There are still many companies that maintain pension plans, but only around half of these are offering the plan to *new* employees. A large number of companies with pensions have decided to stick with the plan, but only for employees who got into the plan a long time ago. Bank of America, for example, still maintains a pension plan for employees, but they closed it to new employees back in 2012. However, there are still some large companies that accept new applicants to their pensions. Most of these are financial institutions, like JPMorgan Chase and Prudential Financial. Most of the plans still open to new employees are the defined benefit version I talked about earlier.

These plans mostly work like this:

- You sign up for the plan and make contributions to it (for example, 6 percent of your salary).

- After five years of working for the company, your plan vests, meaning the money becomes available to you.

🐾 Once you cash out your retirement plan, you usually get around 1.5 to 1.8 percent of your salary for each year you were with the company.

Let's look at an example so that you can see the plan in action, and understand the differences between pensions and the other types of plans we have talked about.

Say you work at a company that offers a defined benefit pension plan, and you sign up right away. Your salary is $80,000 a year. Your plan vests over five years, at which point you decide to leave the company. 1.5 percent of your salary is $1,200, so your pension payout would be $6,000 a year, forever. Now, if you stayed for 15 years, your yearly payout would be $1,200 x 15, or $18,000 a year. And if you spent your entire career at the company, say 40 years, your payout would be $1,200 x 40, or $48,000 a year. Pension payouts usually scale with your salary as well as the number of years with the company, so your benefit would be larger if you got a raise to $100,000 a year after 20 years, for example.

These days, there are federal laws in place that require companies that offer pension plans to keep the fund "topped off." This means companies *have* to keep enough money in the pension fund at all times to cover all future obligations to employees. This can cost companies an extremely large amount of money, which is part of the reason companies are doing away with them in favor of 401(k)s. So, the thing that makes defined benefit pensions so attractive is that at a large company like Prudential, they are exceptionally consistent and secure. You don't have to worry about losing retirement funds if your retirement coincides with a stock market crash that could gut your 401(k). The trade-off is that you can control your 401(k) plan, and it can be worth much, much more than a pension, if your investments earn an exceptional return.

401(K)	PENSION
Subject to market fluctuations	Consistent, secure payouts
Potentially can be worth millions of dollars	Limited by payout structure

401(K)	PENSION
Very common	Less common
Flexible if you change jobs	Often stuck with company offering plan
More control over investments	No control over investments
Matching contributions common	Matching contributions less common

Most companies that have pension plans (including all the ones I mentioned above) also offer 401(k) plans. It is certainly possible to have both. Hell, you could even have a pension plan, a 401(k), and an IRA, if you really wanted to! The problem with this is that most people won't be able to make the most of any single plan if they are chopping up their contributions. Let's say you have all three types of retirement plans, but can only contribute 10 percent of your salary to retirement. If, in order to participate in the pension plan, you are required by your employer to contribute 6 percent of your salary then this means you are only going to be able to put 4 percent of your salary towards the 401(k).

Once you have maxed out your allowable tax deduction, you *can* put money into an IRA, but without taking the deduction. And what have we learned about contributing to a 401(k) and IRA? The more you contribute now, early, the larger your returns will be down the road. If you have confidence in your 401(k) and realize that it has the potential to be worth much, much more than the aggregate of your pension plan benefits, then it might make sense to skip the pension and max out your contributions to the 401(k). However—and...however—if you are willing to commit to a company for life, and see yourself sticking with a single career and employer for 20 or 30 years, then taking the pension plan and supplementing it with a 401(k) could be your best bet to maximize both.

The last major distinction between 401(k)s and pensions has to do with flexibility. As we discussed, if you leave a job, there are *many* options available to you regarding your 401(k). You can roll it over, let it sit, and so on. You don't have most of these options with a pension, especially if you work as a teacher or other public employee. In the vast majority of these cases, pensions stay with the company. If you leave a job, your only option is to take the staggered payout option or lump sum. It *is* possible to rollover some pensions into an IRA, but it can be much more complicated and restrictive than rolling over a 401(k). Getting money out of a pension can be a long, timely process.

My advice is this: if you are offered a pension plan and a 401(k) by your employer, do both if you can. Prioritize the 401(k) unless you see yourself spending a good portion of your career with that employer. After all, the pension is guaranteed money. Remember that a pension plan can be worth it, but only if you are able to make the most of how the benefits are calculated. If you contribute 6 percent of your salary to a pension for five years and nothing to a 401(k), then leave the company after five years, you have drastically scaled back your retirement potential. You have really lost time by contributing to a plan with a very low fixed payout, rather than contributing to one that has (potentially) no upside limit.

THE 42 PERCENT

What if your employer doesn't offer a retirement plan? Well, you are not alone. As of the writing of this book, roughly 42 percent of workers in the private sector in this country don't have access to an employer-backed plan (note that the primary work demographic here is represented by small companies with fewer than 20 employees). Almost half of people don't even have access to a plan they can join. The wonders of technology will change this over time—this is inevitable. (Don't believe me? Just Google Moore's Law.) But the current situation is ridiculous! This puts a lot of people behind the curve, struggling to play catch up. There *are* outside options, like the IRAs we talked about, but these might not be ideal in this situation.

If you defer $5,000 a year into your IRA and $5,000 into your 401(k)—they are both pre-tax, so they might seem similar. They are both easy. You can even set up automatic monthly payments and transfers from your checking account into your IRA. We have the technology! As easy as this is, it still is not as easy as a 401(k). Maybe this is because you only have to make a decision *once* for a 401(k). Once you join the plan, you don't have to worry about transferring money from checking accounts, handpicking each dollar that you want to contribute, and generally acting like you are laundering money in some Swiss bank. Maybe it's because the investment choices are simplified, with a limited "menu" of choices. Maybe they have target-date funds, which are truly "fire and forget." Maybe it is all these things. Whatever the reason, 401(k)s just work more easily. Set it up, and it becomes another line-item deduction on your paycheck. Done.

If that doesn't work, there are some interesting alternatives on the horizon. In early 2017, a number of states began efforts to build state exchanges, where workers could get access to 401(k)s through state governments, using employers as an intermediary. Basically, companies that don't offer plans would be required to offer plans through the state. In many cases, enrollment will be automatic. At the moment these sorts of plans have a lot of potential, but there are many legal issues to resolve before they are reliably available to workers. Keep an eye out for these— Oregon started the first state-run retirement plan in the fall of 2017, and your state might be next!

If you don't want to run off into the retirement fund wilderness, one option is to go to your boss (unless you are the boss) and let him or her know that you, along with your colleagues, would love access to a 401(k). Then demand it! In this day and age, they are super simple and require very little money to get started. The wear and tear on your employer will be minimal. If you and enough of your fellow co-workers fight to be covered, perhaps you can get your employer to wake up and join the twenty-first century. After all, it's your future, and if your boss values your skills, they will do what they can to retain you. Besides, barging into the boss's office is something Jen would do…

OWNING YOUR LIFE

Financial badasses know how to negotiate. They run circles around the rest of us. They talk their way out of overdraft fees, into better loan terms, and into higher salaries and more impressive job titles. They are confident because they can see it all.

What could instill more confidence than the ability to take your future into your own hands, and live on your own terms?

Used to be, you got a job and worked your way up. You stayed in one place, with one company. For life. You settled, bought a house, and really weren't all that different than your neighbors.

Ain't nobody got time for that![2]

With so much to do, and so much to see? Why settle, when you can *set* the terms? Why work from the ground up when thinking ahead will *put* you ahead?

You own your future, and you own your life now. So get more out of your job and your paycheck. Did you know that only about 44 percent of people ask for raises? Can you believe there are that many people who are too tame to *go for it* when the time comes? Smh.

They weren't lying when they said the worst two words you can ask yourself are, "What if?"

What's the worst that can happen? You don't get what you want, you unlock an achievement, and you are better prepared for the next battle.

"You miss 100% of the shots you don't take."

—Wayne Gretzky

—Michael Scott

—George Kroustalis

BALANCING DEBT AND RETIREMENT PLANNING

Debt is everywhere. In some ways, our economy runs off debt. It is very common for people of all walks of life (whether they are in the workforce or not) to be dealing with different kinds of debt: credit cards, car loans, mortgages, medical bills, student loans, and so on. Hopefully you understand by this point the immense power of investing for retirement and starting early. But while you might like to take this

---

2   Not that there is anything wrong with that…if that's what you want.

advice to heart and put as much as possible into your retirement plan, the realities of a debt-ridden society are inescapable. So, what to do?

The first thing to realize is that these debts are all different. The most obvious difference is the fact they might (and probably do) all have different interest rates. When trying to strike a balance between paying your debts and saving for retirement, interest rates are the first thing you should take into consideration. Debts with high interest rates (most likely credit cards and car loans) hurt your financial health the longer they stick around. You should try your best to pay them off sooner. Not only will this mean having more cash on hand in the future to invest, it will also mean improving your credit score. This can give your retirement planning a big boost for a few reasons, some of which have to do with those other types of debt I mentioned.

Many of you are going to be stuck with student loans for a very long time. As we mentioned earlier, the total outstanding student loan debt in the US as of 2017 was $1.48 trillion. More than half of students these days who graduate from college are entering the workforce with some amount of student loan debt. According to the Project on Student Debt, the average student gets that shiny new diploma with over $30,000 in student loans already eating into their future retirement savings. This debt also interferes with the other purchases that keep the economy chugging along: buying houses, buying cars, buying consumer goods like smartphones and lattes and handbags. Thankfully, there are some benefits to paying off short-term, high-interest debts like credit cards that will give you some leeway with these long-term debts.

When you pay off your monthly bill on a credit card, your credit score goes up. It's okay to keep a small balance on a credit card (this means the credit line is *open*), but you should always pay more than the minimum. Lots of cards set you up for failure if you attach too much importance to the minimum payment amount. For example, let's say you have a credit card with a $6,500 balance. Your interest rate is 13 percent. Your minimum monthly payment is $100. That's not bad at all, right? You should have no problem paying off $100 a month. But do you want to pay $100 a month for the next ten years of your life? Even if you only have to pay $100, you should pay more. Paying an extra $50 a month means you will be done in under five years, which is five years that interest isn't accruing. So, always pay more than the minimum monthly payment, keep your credit lines open with a small balance, and watch your score get healthier.

The healthier your credit score, the more bargaining power you have when it comes to consolidating your student loans. Here is how the process works: you graduate from college. You have some student loans. You deal with the monthly payments for a while, live off ramen and hot dogs, and pay off a small credit card balance. Your credit score goes up. From here, having shown the world that you are a responsible borrower, you can approach the lender who holds your loans and consolidate them. This process involves taking out a new loan for the total outstanding amount of the existing loans. The old loans are paid off with the new loan, and you are left with one big loan to make payments on.

This new loan generally comes with a lower interest rate and more flexible payment options. Consolidating student loans is a great way to make payments more manageable, less complicated, and lower. And with the small amount extra you will have each month, you can contribute more to your 401(k)! It's a win-win!

The moral is this: it is important to find a balance between paying off short-term debts so that you can improve your credit score, and finding ways to save so you can increase the amount you contribute to your retirement plan.

WHEN PAYING OFF DEBT IS BETTER THAN INVESTING

A good portion of this book is dedicated to retirement and other investing. Properly investing through a 401(k) or similar plan is extremely important. However, there are times and circumstances where deciding to invest extra money is *not* the right move, and this has to do with the constricting effect of debt on your investing potential. Remember the "Einstein" quote? Well, compounding can work against you, and things like mortgages and student loans can put a damper on your ability to make meaningful contributions to your 401(k). If you have large amounts of debt, it is an excellent idea to get rid of them sooner rather than later, and this can mean making the hard decision to increase your monthly payments before increasing your retirement contributions.

We can look at an unlikely example to get this point across. Here are the facts:

- You are thirty years old. No, that's not the unlikely part, bear with me!
- You have $60,000 in student loan debt.
- You have a 401(k) that is worth $60,000.
- You are paying $300 a month for the loans, and are contributing the same amount to your 401(k).
- Your interest rate on the student loans is 5 percent, and your 401(k) is returning the same annualized rate.
- You plan on retiring when you turn sixty-seven.

Got all that? Now, at this rate you will pay off your student loans in thirty-five years, and will end up paying $69,275 in interest, for a grand total of $129,275 paid. Once you pay off your student loan at age sixty-five, you will be able to put the $300 you were putting towards that, and start putting it towards your 401(k). Contributing $300 a month for thirty-five years, then contributing $600 a month for another two years (to bring you up to age 67) will result in your 401(k) being worth $756,787.78 when you retire. Man, we would be lost without calculators.

Now we come to the unlikely part. Through some crazy luck, you end up winning the lottery, and the payout after taxes is exactly $60,000. So, you face an interesting question. Is it better to use your lottery winnings to pay off the student loan all at once and contribute $600 a month to your 401(k) for thirty-five years, or is it better to invest that $60,000 in your 401(k)[3], and keep the $300/$300 payment system the same? To make this example easier to understand, we are just going to conveniently ignore the limits to annual 401(k) contributions and let you put it all into your fund at once. So, everything *else* is the same, but instead of having a 401(k) at age 30 that is worth $60,000, you have one that is worth $120,000.

Let me bust out the calculator again. Making those same contributions ($300 a month for thirty-five years, then $600 a month for two years) to a 401(k) worth $120,000 will result in your 401(k) being worth $1,121,672.20. Okay, you might think that is pretty awesome! You made an extra $60,000 contribution, and got back $364,884.42! However, if you had used your lottery winnings to pay off the student loan and

---

3   We are going to assume, hypothetically, that you can make this one-time lump sum deposit for the purposes of this example. In reality, you cannot do this.

then put $600 a month towards your 401(k) from age 30 onwards, your 401(k) would be worth $1,133,193.15. Prioritizing the student loan over the 401(k) in this case means you would have over $11,000 more when you retire. More importantly, you didn't end up paying the loan company that extra $69,275 in interest! We are talking about an $80,000 swing here, which is a big deal. And on top of that, you will have a killer credit score!

The lesson here is that when you get a raise, or find yourself with extra cash some other way, it is a good idea to prioritize paying off very large and/or high-interest debts before you think about saving more, especially if the interest rate on the loan or credit card is north of 10 percent. I'm not saying you should completely ignore retirement investing if you have debt. You can certainly manage both. But you want to *earn* interest as much as possible, and pay interest as little as possible. This means getting rid of high-interest debt every chance you get!

SUCCESS BY A THOUSAND STEPS

There is an old saying that talks about "death by a thousand cuts." Historically, this was a nasty way of dealing with captured enemies in ancient China. Nowadays, the phrase is a metaphor for the slow demise of something by a series of small, successive mistakes or setbacks. We aren't going to dwell on the negative aspects here. Just the opposite! In much the same manner, modern financial planning can bring you success though small, sequential *good moves* that slowly build into a picture of overall financial health. We have already seen with the magic of compounding how small contributions can yield amazing results over time. In everyday life, there are ways you can make tiny contributions to your financial behaviors and patterns that will net you results that are just as amazing!

These small contributions are broken down into the following categories:

- Employment benefits
- Turning downtime into investing time
- Earning while spending
- Squeezing in extra work

Employment Benefits

Companies offer a wide range of benefits to their employees. These vary from company to company, but if you know what to look for and pay attention during orientation, you can find yourself equipped with many tools that will help you save and earn money. The federal government has allowed for certain benefits, sometimes called "fringe benefits," to be tax exempt in much that same way that 401(k) contributions are. Not all benefits will be tax exempt, but that doesn't make them unimportant.

Some of the most common benefits deal with getting to and from work. These transportation benefits can offer you massive savings on the necessary costs associated with getting to work, and are a good first step towards success through a thousand steps. And don't worry, there won't *actually* be a thousand of them. Ain't nobody got time for that.

Transportation benefits are offered for both those who drive to work on their own and those who take public transportation. An example of the former is the IRS policy on reimbursement for gas, the standard rate for which is 53.5 cents per mile. Employers can offer more or less than this, and some might not offer any at all; figuring out whether a prospective employer does offer it should be a part of any job search where you are going to be forced to drive yourself to work. There are even more substantial benefits for those who take public transportation. For example, the Washington D.C. Metro system has a program called SmartBenefits. In this program, pre-tax money that you earn is applied to a card that you can use for Metro and bus fare, as well as pay for parking at Metro stations. The fact that it is automated makes it even sweeter, like we learned in a previous section. It only takes a few paychecks for you to not really notice the difference in pay, and you don't have to worry about manually putting aside money for transportation. These commuter benefits are easy to take advantage of, and it is comforting to know that you are saving a small amount of money just by going to work!

Other benefits that employers often offer on a pre-tax basis are connected to:

- Employee discounts on merchandise
- Use of a company car or paid cell phone plan
- Moving expense reimbursement
- Awards pertaining to exemplary service or safety records

These benefits represent a win–win for both employees and employers. Employers are able to offer prospective workers a more attractive package, which serves to both draw in new talent and retain an existing workforce. The federal government assists companies in offering these plans, up to certain dollar amounts, as a way to stimulate job growth and the overall expansion of the economy. Employees get very obvious perks; they pay less for merchandise, they pay less for commuting costs, they can more easily relocate for job reasons, they can earn bonuses, and so on.

ESP

Not the telekinetic ability, unfortunately. Employee stock purchase plans are another major benefit that some employers offer. They exist kind of in the sweet spot between the different benefits and investment plans we have talked about. ESPPs are a way for a company to compensate employees for their work by letting them purchase stock in the company. These purchases generally have favorable terms and are extremely easy to make. For one thing, you don't have to go through a broker or anything like that; ESPPs work through payroll deductions, usually after-tax. When you get into the program, you can purchase stock in the company through an automated process. In theory, you want the stock to rise in value, which means that the company will have to be successful. This should encourage you to work hard and do your part to make sure the company is efficient and healthy. In short, you have some skin in the game!

There are different types of ESPPs. Some offer purchasing options on a pre-tax basis (like your 401(k) contributions), and some have more strict limits on how much stock you can purchase than others. Often, ESPPs have *purchase periods*, which are stretches of time where stock is open for sale. It all varies from company to company. Below, you will find some guidelines that will help you navigate your employer's ESPP, if they have one.

- ♥ **Pay close attention to purchase periods, and the price at which stock is available for purchase.** It is common for purchase periods to be broken up into sections a few months long, and employees generally have a choice: they can choose to buy on the *last* day of the previous section, or the *first* day of the upcoming section. The nice part is that you can choose to buy stock at the lower of those two prices, meaning you essentially get a discount not available to outside investors.

- ☛ **Make sure you understand the requirements for participating in the ESPP.** Much like with 401(k)s, you will have to figure out contribution limits and minimums, and make sure that you are able to afford contributing to the ESPP. Most ESPPs have a minimum contribution of 2 percent of your salary, with a 15 percent maximum. So, these plans can be very beneficial, but make sure you can afford it! If you are contributing 6 percent of your salary to your 401(k), 3 percent to the ESPP, and 4 percent to your IRA...well, that starts to add up!

- ☛ **Understand when (and if!) you should cash out your stock. This can be a complicated decision.** Remember when we talked about diversification and how it is one of the keys to successful investing? Well, if you pump a significant amount of your salary into an ESPP, you are by definition not diversifying. You are putting all your eggs in one basket, in a way. If the company gets hit with a big scandal or gets bumped off by a competitor, you run the risk of losing everything you put in. In order to protect yourself against this, I recommend not contributing more than 5 percent of your salary to an ESPP. Now, if the stock goes way up in price, and your shares comprise more than 5 percent of your total investments, I would recommend selling some off in order to bring your investment commitment via ESPP down to 5 percent.

- ☛ **Taxes!** You don't have to pay taxes on your ESPP earnings until you sell. If you do sell, be aware that this kind of capital gain is specially treated when you have to pay your taxes. There are a lot of variables to consider, like balancing the *cost* price of the shares and the *sell* price. More often than not, you will end up using a host of intimidating tax forms. But don't worry, TurboTax or a tax professional will get you sorted out. I won't go into the details here, but I just wanted to make sure you are aware of the tax situation!

Let's close out this section with a story. I don't want you to assume this will happen to you, but it's still a fun story and gives an example of the power of ESPPs and similar plans. Way back in 1999, a woman took a job at a company as an in-house masseuse. Her job was to relieve employee tension with the power of massage. She didn't make that much money—less than $500 a week. However, she was given stock options with the company. She decided to go for it.

Well, that company was a little place called Google. A few years later, she cashed out her stock for millions of dollars and went right into retirement. She went from giving massages to getting them. Now, this is a rare, once-in-a-lifetime success story. It might not happen to you. But just in case you end up working for the next Google...sign up for the ESPP, invest a modest amount, and see where it takes you!

Turning Downtime into Investing Time

The information age (just a fancy way of saying, isn't the Internet neat?!) has given us more tools than ever before to squeeze out earnings where and when you least expect it. Back in the day, investing was time-consuming and complicated. If you wanted to purchase shares, you had to contact a broker and place your order over...gasp...a landline! The broker would then pass on your order information to the trade floors and exchanges. You really had to know your stuff, and you had to act quickly to get your orders through at the right time. There was a meaningful barrier of entry up until the 1990s, when various companies started offering online services that approximated the investor-broker-exchange dynamic. These gradually emerged in two forms: those which paired orders with market maker firms (basically, these firms match sell and buy asks together, hoping to make a profit on the margin between the quoted price and purchase offer), and those that give individual investors direct access to exchanges.

As time went on, these online tools became more sophisticated. Nowadays, investing online is a full-fledged experience. Research, real-time prices, and countless other tools are included in most online brokerage platforms. These days, anyone can be an investor!

There are many different online brokerages to choose from, with slightly different requirements and capabilities. The important thing to remember is that all of them can help you invest in something that grabs your attention, allowing you to earn money in the background while you go about your everyday life. Here are the main elements to keep an eye out for when deciding on an online brokerage:

Initial Funding

Some firms require you to put money up front when starting your account. Essentially, you are putting money into their system from day one, which can then be used to invest in a wide variety of stocks, mutual funds, and more. Others will let you start an account with a $0 balance, because they realize some people will want to try out the service before actually committing to it. Then, when you have familiarized yourself with the layout and are confident, you can begin investing money. Most brokers *do* have an initial funding requirement, but if you are looking to get into the game as cheaply as possible, there are still plenty available that do not. And check out the benefits for brokers that require initial funding. Some offer a certain number of free trades as an added perk to funding an account!

Transaction Fees

Brokers need to make money too, and the most common way they do this is by charging a fee for transactions. If you want to invest in a certain company and purchase stock in them, your online broker will charge you for making it all happen. These fees take many difference forms and are probably what you should research first when deciding on a broker. These fees, called "commissions," are generally in the ballpark of $5-$10, with some variance on either side. If you are just dabbling in trading and make one or two trades a month, this is very manageable. But if you plan on spending more time and money on trading and end up performing a number of transactions a month, be aware that you might end up spending hundreds, if not thousands, of dollars per year.

Additional Fees

When you sign up for an online broker service, make sure you read the fine print. There can be a number of additional fees besides transaction fees! Some brokers charge fees to close accounts, to transfer money out of accounts, or if your account is inactive for a certain amount of time. Also be aware that some features you might want could come with extra fees attached.

Premium Features

Online brokers have a *ton* of extra features available. These include, but are not limited to, real-time stock prices, historic research and tools that will let you see how hypothetical purchases would have panned out, goal-based guide tools, educational content, tax help, live customer service, discounts if you are a very active trader, and free introductory periods. It is very important that you figure out what your goals are and what features you would like. And it's not just stocks you can trade these days. You can trade options, currencies, and even cryptos!

A Tale of Three Brokers

The first thing that Jen was sure of was that she was dreaming. That was the only possible explanation for the dog in a top hat that was standing alongside her. Jen looked around, and it became clear she and the dog were in a sort of marketplace. The dog was flipping from screen to screen on a huge smartphone, totally ignoring her.

"What can I do for you?" she asked a bit gruffly. She had been up way into the night trying to figure out what online broker to choose. She was jet-lagged, having just returned from an extended European trip, and really wanted to set something up so that she could get back to her life without micromanaging her investments.

"You tell me," the dog replied. "I'm your creation. Can I get Twitter on this thing?"

Jen looked around and asked, "Where are we?"

"It appears to be an alley of broker salesmen. You must have been doing some *fascinating* reading right before nodding off," the dog said drily.

And so it was. There were all sorts of tables set up in the alley, and the three closest to her had signs up that advertised their services. "Cheap Trades!" "Anything You Can Shake a Stick At!" "Any Service is Better Than No Service!"

Jen was intrigued and walked up to the first table. Behind it was a young man with gigantic glasses, wearing a cheap suit and a bow tie.

"Ah, I could tell you were a go-getter from the moment you... materialized...down in that alley. You have come to the right place. I offer the *cheapest* trading services you can imagine. Only a dollar per trade, no questions asked!"

Jen thought for a moment. This could work to her advantage. Perhaps the overload of information she had uncovered in her research was simpler here. Sometimes people just need a fresh perspective to understand a problem. She shrugged; she had nothing better to do, and she was already here.

"That sounds pretty nice," she said. "What sort of tools does your service offer? Can I see historic prices of stocks on your platform?"

"Well, er," the salesman said hesitantly, "we kind of prefer our customers do that on their own. After all, you know what you're doing, right? You wouldn't be looking for a broker if you weren't educated on the market already!"

This suddenly didn't sound like too great of a deal to Jen. It sounded to her like the reason the trade fees were so cheap was that this particular broker didn't offer any sort of extra features to help her make wise investing choices.

"Sounds a bit like a scam to me," whispered the dog. Now he was taking selfies.

"I heard that! No, it isn't a scam. We just like to offer cheap trades to people who are willing to do most of their market research on their own, or only have a little bit of money to get started with."

Jen considered this, and walked on to the next table. The dog followed.

Behind this table was an extremely well-dressed woman. She had pearl earrings and a vintage Rolex watch. Her table was also very fancy, more of a giant hardwood desk, and was covered with an immense number of papers filled with equations, facts and figures, and charts.

"I can tell you have potential to do some *real* investing," she began with a smile. "With my service, you get everything that oaf doesn't offer. We will give you historical information on prices, as well as real-time prices, up-to-the-minute news, and more. You name it, and we have it!"

This sounded good to Jen. Almost too good. Armed with all of this knowledge, of course she would be able to make a killing investing! She glanced at the dog to see what he thought. He shook his head and went back to playing a Flappy Bird clone.

"I don't know if this is for you," he muttered. "Ask about what the catch is."

Jen returned to the woman, and asked, "So, how much is it going to cost me to use your service? You have an awful lot of features, which is nice, but it can't be free."

"I knew you were savvy! Couldn't pass anything over on you!" the woman said, with just a hint of trepidation in her voice. "To start off with my service, you need to fund your account with $10,000. From there, each of your transactions will have a fee of $9.99. But for someone like you who has the look of an investor, and with all the extra stuff we provide, I'm sure you will agree that it is worth it."

Well, that stopped Jen in her tracks. She certainly didn't have $10,000 to spend on something like this, and even with all the information in the world, $9.99 per trade seemed pretty steep to her.

"I knew it!" said the dog. "Maybe in a few years, once you have some experience, this will be a better choice. But not now. In the meantime, help me find an outlet, I'm running low."

Reluctantly, Jen agreed. It certainly seemed like a quality service, but there was a pretty big barrier of entry. It might be better to try something else out, since she was just starting as an investor and just wanted to dip her toes in the water. Her excitement dwindling, she walked on to the last table.

On this table were a modest number of items. There was one tablet with what looked like some real-time trading stats, and another that looked like it was advertising an app of some kind.

"All right," she said, "let's hear the bad news."

"No bad news here," said the young man behind the table. He was wearing a polo and some khakis. He wasn't going to win any fashion awards or pop in as an extra on a hip hop video, but he seemed trustworthy.

"We offer a little bit of everything. I have some nice tools that you can see here on the table, which will give you enough information to navigate the modern marketplace, but nothing that will overwhelm you with information while charging a premium to do so. If you want to get some middle-of-the-road information with reasonable prices, you have come to the right place."

The dog had given up on his phone, which was now completely dead.

"Perfect!" he said. "This seems like just the place! You have a spare charger?"

Jen had to agree. She asked a few more questions and found out that all of the basics were covered: she could watch the market in real-time, didn't have to fund the service up front, and the fee per trade was half that of the well-dressed women with the watch. Soon enough, Jen discovered that her confusion was gone; she knew just what to do. She handed the dog the charger that she found in her dream-pocket, and woke up.

The moral of this story should be obvious. If you are like Jen and just want to get a taste of investing, you want to try out a simple online broker that has modest prices. You aren't going to take to it like a fish in water on the first day. If you go with a high-end broker with all the bells and whistles without first trying something easier, you're gonna have a bad time. This doesn't mean that high-end brokers are bad (they can actually be pretty awesome), but when you are just getting your toes wet, something simpler might be better. But you are smart too, and know that anything that *sounds* too good to be true is probably too good to be free! So keep calm and research on. Take your time, and following the guidelines established before this story, choose something that suits where you are financially, educationally, and personally.

There's an App for That! (Of course there is...)

We use our smartphones for everything these days, and your financial activity should be no exception! Most of the major online brokers, and some smaller ones, have high-quality smartphone apps so that you can monitor your accounts on the go. Now, this can be hugely convenient, especially if you get really into online investing. However, constantly monitoring your investments can cause some psychological wear and tear. Remember the Sleep Factor? Well, some of us sleep better when we don't know how the market is doing every second of every day, since everybody gets at least a little bummed when their investments drop in value. The same rules for the Sleep Factor apply to monitoring your investments on an app. Determine your level of comfort when it comes to the ebbs and flows of the market, and discipline yourself not to make rash decisions in the face of market volatility.

Tony Robbins is a well-known businessman, investor, and author. He has said in numerous interviews that the key to muscling through a drop in the market is to take yourself out of it. Detach yourself emotionally. Be ruthlessly unshakeable. Don't tamper with your plan just because you temporarily lost some gains. Sound familiar? It's the exact same lesson from Warren Buffett about perseverance and calmness being the key to *net-saving*. So if you don't take my word for it, take theirs! After all, they have made a little bit of money employing this strategy!

Niche Apps

On top of banking apps and apps for online broker services, there are a number of niche investing and finance apps that have made an appearance in recent years. I will talk about a few of them briefly so you have an idea of what is available.

Acorns is a clever app that lets you work investing into your everyday purchases. It works by linking your payment methods (bank account, debit card, and credit card) to its system. When you buy something with one of those payment methods, your purchase is rounded up to the nearest dollar. So if you buy a coffee for $2.50, Acorns rounds the purchase up to $3.00. That extra $0.50 is then invested in a wide variety of stocks and bonds. The Acorn system is one of micro-transactions... and is the very definition of success by a thousand steps. One of the elements that makes this app such a terrific choice for anyone interested in starting to invest is the fact that the investments Acorns puts your money towards are *diversified index funds*. (Remember those?) This way you don't need to worry too much about whether to invest in this stock or that stock...you are investing in the entire markets.

The other big way that Acorns can get you into investing is the fact that the investment amounts are small and wrapped up in purchases you are already going to make. This means that you will barely notice the missing money. You are investing without having to specifically allocate money into an online broker, and you aren't paying $6.95 per transaction. Instead, you pay a consistent monthly fee that has no hidden surprises. The experience is streamlined, easy, and works, making it an ideal starting point for the budding investor.

For social media savvy investors, Benzinga is a great resource. This app offers real-time stock prices, news, and customizable lists for your most-watched stocks. Social media capabilities are baked into the app as well, which let you send and receive tweets for market developments and share using multiple social media networks. This is a great supplemental app for any investor, and is particularly geared towards people who are regular tweeters, likers, and sharers.

The last investing app I'll mention is perhaps the first one you should try, and one of the most fun. Stock Market Simulator lets you test out investing by giving you a pool of fake money, and letting you invest your $10,000 in play money in a simulated stock market. This fake market is a mirror of the real stock market, so you can actually get some legitimate investing experience under your belt without risking any real money. You can track your investments down to the minute, just like you would be able to with a real online broker app, and rest easy knowing you are just practicing! I should mention that you shouldn't use this as a tool for actual investing. This is just so that you get first-hand experience of market volatility and get used to the ups and downs, 'cause you will experience them.

Earning While Spending

Acorns is one example where daily spending can earn you money down the line. There are few other ways to accomplish this, the most obvious being credit card reward systems. In order to attract more customers, credit card companies offer benefits based on how much, and where, you spend. These take many different forms, the main ones being cash back bonuses, airline miles, and hotel rewards. As you use your credit cards, you earn points towards these various rewards. For example, some credit cards might offer 5,000 mile bonuses to cardholders who spend $1,000 on their card within a certain number of months. Others might offer a fraction of a percent in cash back for every dollar spent, with bonus payouts if you buy from certain vendors like Amazon. Cash back bonuses accumulate, and you can either use them to pay off some of the credit card balance, or get a debit card that has your rewards balance on it.

As a matter of fact, if you put the time in (and you should!), credit card rewards systems can be a bit of job on their own. It isn't uncommon for people to have 10 or more credit cards, so that they can reap the benefits of rewards systems. Some people even pay for entire vacations with rewards points! If navigating over a dozen monthly bill due dates, interest rates, and reward points sounds like fun to you, then bust out Excel and get to crunching the numbers. While many young people successfully juggle large credit card balances over many different cards, I should put in due diligence here by suggesting you don't get into this game unless you have done your research and know what you are doing!

When applying for credit cards, it is definitely best to make a low interest rate a priority, unless you are one of the thrill seekers I mentioned above. You want the best deal you can get when it comes to interest, especially if you are looking at your first credit card. A solid rewards structure is still a meaningful perk, however, so make sure you do the research and find out what rewards are offered. This might take some digging, as credit card reward systems have gotten pretty complicated over the years and the information might not be obviously available.

Another way you can get a little extra from consistent spending is with a store credit card. These generally don't have the best terms and usually have high interest rates and low limits. For that reason, I can't wholeheartedly recommend them. However, they can be situationally useful, and some do come with genuinely nice perks. There are two types of store credit cards. Some are partnered with established credit card companies like VISA and MasterCard. Because of this partnership, you can use the card basically anywhere. Other cards can only be used at the issuing store. They are essentially cards that offer credit just at Macy's, or Home Depot, or wherever you got them.

Store credit cards have a low barrier of entry, so if you are just starting to build your credit, they can be an excellent way to get your foot in the door and demonstrate that you are a responsible borrower. This is probably their main perk. Building credit, as we have seen, is a key part of attaining financial freedom. In addition to jump-starting your credit history, these cards offer additional incentives. You almost always get a store discount when buying merchandise at the issuing store, and you can also get access to things like exclusive coupons and free shipping on orders. The Amazon VISA card, for example, gives you 3 percent back on all purchases on Amazon, 1 percent back on all other purchases, a $50 gift card just for signing up, and no annual fee. And who doesn't spend a ton on Amazon already?

Make a list of all the features you want in a card, taking into account your spending habits, how much you are able to pay monthly towards your balance (informed by the saving and spending chart we worked through earlier in the book), and your tolerance for interest rates. If you do a lot of freelance landscaping, for example, and spend a lot of money at Home Depot, then maybe a credit card there is good for you. I'll leave you with this rule of thumb: avoid anything with an APR of over 20 percent. That level of interest is just too high to manage if you are just starting out in your credit history. The landscape is so large that there is an emerging industry dedicated to maxing out credit card reward points.

FUTURE-PROOF

A financial badass knows how to do the things she wants (eating out, having a nice phone or computer, going on vacations and to concerts, etc.) without having to worry and without having to apologize. This is because she has thought through her savings, understands her priorities, and knows that there is no one-size-fits-all solution to managing purchases. Traditional purchases for previous generations when they were your age (like a house) aren't standard anymore. You have flexibility, and you want to hang on to it. So you can tweak your monthly expenditures to future-proof your financial fun, and have a ton of fun in the meantime.

You have to be future-proof. Handle your shit now, so that you won't be vulnerable later. Think of this like having great defense. Sure, we all want to to shoot like Steph Curry and throw up 80+ points a game and blow out the other guys. You can win a lot this way, but defense wins championships!

Take risks, but save too, because the most successful investors will be the ones who are the most versatile. And of course, you can't invest if you have nothing *to* invest.

A financial badass exists on the bleeding edge. Whether it comes to consumer tech or bitcoin, today's under-30 crowd knows its way across the digital landscape. If there is an app for something (and there always is), they use it. If there is a lifehack, they've found it. If there is a breaking news story, they are knee-deep in comments and analysis before the story has even reached mainstream news sources.

So this book might teach you a few things, but that isn't as important as waking the badass within you; you will find out more on your own, using the tools you have mastered and your instincts, after you finish this book and go back out into the world.

"There are no traffic jams along the extra mile."

— Roger Staubach

Squeezing in Extra Work

There are more opportunities today than ever before to supplement your income with odd jobs. This is largely due to the power of the internet and the fact that we can do so much with our smartphones. Let's take a look at a few popular services that can help you make a buck here and there in addition to your primary source of income.

How many times did you use Uber last month? It has been a long time since a company or service has rolled around that has shaken up an industry the way Uber has. For those of you who don't know how Uber works, think of it as an alternative to taking a taxi. Everyday people, driving their own cars, pick up people who need rides. Passengers pay for the trip, and the fee is split between Uber and the driver. It is all done through a very streamlined app that makes it easy for passengers and drivers to meet, for payments to be processed, and for you to review and rate your experience. There are some requirements for being an Uber driver. You must be at least 21 years old with three years of driving experience, have a 4-door sedan or equivalent vehicle that is newer than 2001, and pass a background check, You also have to meet the usual federal and state requirements for operating a motor vehicle: a valid driver's license and proof of insurance, proper registration, and a Social Security number. Once you have all that out of the way, you can start making money in your downtime!

If you have a typical nine-to-five job, but have plenty of energy at the end of the work day and don't mind chatting with strangers, Uber could work out great for you. In metropolitan areas, Uber drivers often make a respectable $15-$25 an hour, sometimes much more. Of course, it is also possible to hit a slow night and not make much money. Uber is also fairly competitive, and lots of people are giving it a try. The flexibility of working your own hours, and the fact that people always need rides, at all hours of the day and night, make Uber a unique way of making cash. And by employing an extra tip at the end of this section, you can make this extra cash work even more in your favor.

Another popular service that people use to make extra money is TaskRabbit. This is a social media hub where people can post ads for work they need done. Someone might need a dozen fancy cupcakes ordered, picked up, and delivered for a birthday party, or a college student might need help editing a term paper. The tasks are endless and varied. The ad posters attach a price they are willing to pay for the service, and then people can pick up the jobs through the website or smartphone app. Like with Uber, there are some legal requirements. You need to be 21, have a bank account and credit card, and live in one of the areas where TaskRabbit operates (many major cities in the United States). You'll also need a smartphone to manage your tasks. TaskRabbit can be a great way to meet new people, do new things, and exercise your skills in ways you might not be able to in your day-to-day work. And you make money the whole time! You can also branch out into freelance delivery: UberEats, Amazon Flex, and other services pay competitive hourly rates and give you the chance to work when you have extra time.

WHY IS THIS IMPORTANT?

Now we get to the real meat on how success by a thousand steps can happen, and how these lessons on spending, saving, and investing, powered by modern technological tools, can make you *dangerous*. Let's pull it all together.

You have a nine-to-five job that pays you a reasonable salary. You signed up for your company's 401(k) plan and are well on your way to retirement. You have divided your paychecks into three accounts, so that you have flexible money (aka Freedom Fund), are saving towards long-term goals, and are building an emergency fund. You have done your homework and gotten commuter benefits, making it cheaper to get to and from work. You have signed up for Acorns, so all your little purchases are slowly building in value in a global investing market.

You have smartly started to build your credit history and are earning back cold hard cash from your credit card purchases. You drive for Uber on Friday and Saturday nights, making a couple hundred dollars. Just make sure you leave one evening free for a nice dinner at Nobu! On the weekend, you do odd jobs on TaskRabbit and make a couple hundred more by picking things up, dropping things off, and maybe even fixing a leaky faucet or two. You will be a regular Superman or Wonder Woman!

If Jen starts a job that offers a 401(k) but cannot maximize her contributions (up to the legal limit), she is missing some serious earning potential. Maybe she just isn't able to afford it, or isn't comfortable with it. Now, imagine she takes the advice in this section and starts squeezing in extra work. Her cash back rewards and earnings from Uber and Amazon Flex cover most of her groceries for a month. Acorns fills in some cracks as well, and she is able to free up more of her pre-tax salary dollars to contribute to her 401(k). Her employer matches her contribution. Let's say she does this consistently, month after month. Soon she is chucking money at her monthly expenses from all directions, chipping away at them so that she can invest more powerfully. This means she can hit her contribution limit, earn as much free money as her employer can give her, and start taking huge strides towards being loaded after exiting the working world. She has turned into the LeBron James of retirement planning, capable of doing it all.

CONGRATULATIONS, YOU HAVE MORE THAN DOUBLED YOUR NET WORTH AT RETIREMENT AGE!

Think about it…you have the tools and the motivation to turn free time into staggering gains through the miracle of compounding, and it was all done through tiny, easy, incremental steps. One of the big takeaways here is this:

Compounding and incremental contributions to retirement and investment accounts can turn any amount of money into a powerhouse of earning potential on a long enough timeline.

BEING A REAL ADULT

So, you're an investor. You're a net-saver. You're on the road to financial independence, and you feel on top of the world. But when you make money, sometimes you gotta pay the piper—in this case, the piper is the federal government. Yep, I'm talking about taxes. They can be a pain and they can be complicated, especially for a dangerous investor like you, a wizard who is pulling in cash left and right from multiple places. Luckily for you, technology strikes again! You have a wealth of tools available to you that will make this infamously difficult process a breeze. Before we get into those tools, how about a brief overview of what sorts of things you will have to do to keep the IRS off your back? I'm not a CPA, so I am going to stop right here with giving tax advice. Instead, I'll talk about technology and logistics.

You can process everything yourself, by hand. This is the free option, but it is the most difficult, and you run the risk of making a mistake that can prove to be costly. It is also time-consuming, and wouldn't you rather use that time doing something fun, making money, or doing literally anything else? Of course you would!

The second option is to hire a professional to do your taxes for you. Once you have everything together, you can contact H&R Block or some other company, dump the papers on someone's desk (metaphorically speaking), and pay them to do the dirty work for you. This is certainly a viable option, and the one that runs the least risk of resulting in an error. It is also the most expensive, with accountants often charging a couple hundred a pop.

The third option is using an online service to help you file your taxes, and exists somewhere in the middle. These services require you to get all your information together and put it into their system, which will then guide you step by step through the process. The actual hard stuff, like looking up tax brackets, calculating earnings, and doing the math for deductions, is done in the background by a computer, but you still have to put information in piece by piece. Since you are doing some of the legwork when using a service like this, the prices is, as expected, right between free and what you would pay an accountant. The online tax-processing leader, TurboTax, offers tax services that range from $0 for simple 1040EZ filings to around $100 for detailed filings that take into account investment earnings, deductions, and business expenses.

I recommend using TurboTax, or a similar service that is a viable option. After all, we already use online banking services, smartphone apps for investing, and automated systems for direct deposit. Why travel back to the Dark Ages and do our taxes with pen and paper? Online tax services have some great tools that will guide you, in easy language, through the complex webs of deductions that would otherwise take either a lot of time or a lot of money to do.

YOU GOT THAT AMBITION...

The job market these days can be brutal. Fierce competition and the aftermath of the 2008 crisis can make it difficult to find a job. If you do find a job, getting a competitive salary is a whole other challenge. Let's hammer it home one more time: a little bit more money now is a lot more money down the road. You want to maximize your earning power when you are young and full of energy, and a key part of professional life that isn't talked about enough these days is the ability to negotiate a strong salary and raises.

This is important because, obviously, the larger your salary, the more you can contribute to a 401(k), IRA, ESPP...you name it. These are valuable tools in your financial arsenal, and in order to make them work for you, you have to work for them by getting that salary you are worth. Learning these skills isn't easy; let's go over some of the basics so that you are able to go into any job interview or performance evaluation guns blazing!

- **Step One: Take stock of your skills.** Take a look at your education history and performance, your previous jobs, volunteer work, and hobbies. Identify what makes you, you! If you volunteered at a homeless shelter one summer and had an easy time talking with strangers, make sure you can describe that quality to a possible employer in terms of your value to a team and your ability to work and communicate with anyone to get the job done. If you got great grades in math in college, and less good grades in English, be able to describe your "proven analytic skills" and "attention to detail." Focus on your strengths. You have skills and a mindset that are uniquely yours, so draw attention to them!

"Every battle is won before it is ever fought."

—Sun Tzu

- **Step Two: Go in prepared.** It's very important that you know the lay of land when you head into an interview. Make sure you know what salaries are attached to positions at other companies similar to the one you are interviewing for. Do the research, and figure out just how valuable you are in the context of the greater marketplace. In fact, you should be so prepared on this front that you should have a dollar figure in mind before you walk through the door!

- **Step Three: Cover your bases.** It is important to get all the necessary information out of a job interview and job offer. As you know from reading this book, there may be hidden perks to the salary. Ask about whether the salary is base pay only, and try to find out about ESPPs, options, or sign-on bonuses. Ask if the job offer will come in writing, what the start date is, and when benefits become available to new hires.

- **Step Four: Don't commit too early.** If you get a job and salary offer, don't agree to it right away. I know the temptation will be huge to just say "yes," but you could gain quite a bit by slowing down and counteroffering. At the most basic level, what does a job and salary offer tell you? That the company *wants* you to work for them. Out of all the candidates that may have applied for the position, they decided you were the one they wanted. This means momentum is on your side: you can leverage their admission that they want you into a larger salary. Be tactful about this, and don't just come out with a point-blank counteroffer. Tell them you will consider their offer, and then get back to them by saying how enthusiastic you are about the opportunity, and then present justification for a higher salary. Make it clear that you have done your research and know the job market. Above all, don't take too much time getting back to them. They aren't going to wait around forever for you to make up your mind.

- **Not really a step, but important anyway!** Most people don't negotiate for raises and higher salaries. They do this for many reasons: fear of receiving "no" for an answer, fear of retribution on the part of the employer, and so on. What most people don't realize is that the vast majority of employers have no problem with prospective hires negotiating for higher pay. In fact, according to a number of surveys, many employers *expect* to receive a counteroffer, and then never get them! So don't be scared of rejection or suffering consequences. Most companies expect salary negotiations to take place, and they almost never take back a job offer if the hire comes back with higher salary requirements. The possible rewards are high, and the downsides minimal; just make sure you are professional, thoughtful, and polite, and demonstrate why you are the right person for the job.

THE REST OF THE STORY

We've spent a lot of time talking about saving, 401(k)s, and investing. You might think that this is all there is to retirement planning, but luckily for you, that is not the case. There are several other factors that complete the picture of a successful retirement that are meant to supplement your own retirement savings. But first, let's talk about goals. Goals were a big part of our breakdown of smartly managing your monthly income, when it comes to things like buying a house and building an emergency fund. Retirement is no different. It is important to have concrete goals when planning for your departure from the working world.

The main thing to figure out is this: how much money do I need to save up in order to check out of the working world, and do it comfortably? Of course, this is going to vary from person to person, so there isn't one set dollar figure. But people have different spending habits, different expectations for meals, entertainment, and housing, and obviously retire to many different parts of the world. All these factors should be taken into consideration when trying to guesstimate what dollar amount you should shoot for.

Like we said earlier, you're not even thinking about this yet, but never fear, because there is an underlying philosophy to this process that serves as an excellent starting point. Let's assume that everyone would like to retire and have more or less the same standard of living that they had when they were working. After all, you don't want to retire and then have to completely change the things you do for fun because you can't afford your old habits anymore. You don't want to have to buy cheaper groceries, or take fewer vacations, or get rid of your car, or buy cheaper clothes. What you want is to *own* your retirement; you want to live comfortably and with the same swag as before! This is a natural goal, and one that is very attainable, especially if you plan ahead of time.

When you retire, you might not have to pay for a lot of the things that you used to. For example, if you were an HVAC technician, you don't have to worry anymore about buying new tools every few months. In a nutshell, when you retire you can find yourself with fewer costs because you no longer have to sustain a professional life. There is a certain balance here: you will have to live off the foundation you laid throughout your working life and will no longer have a paycheck, but the costs of day-to-day living are probably going to go down. On the flipside, some people spend *more* in retirement than they did when they were working. There is no one-size-fits-all equation.

Taking into account these factors, the common wisdom is that in order to retire and maintain the standard of living you were accustomed to while you were working, most studies show you should have access to 70 percent to 100 percent of your former salary each year. Think of this as a general rule of thumb to get you on the right track. So if you were making $60,000 a year in the years leading up to retirement, you should aim for having at least $42,000 available to you each year. If you were making $100,000, aim for at least $70,000. $200,000, at least $140,000. You get the idea.

Now, no one knows how long they are going to live, so we can't really set a specific figure to our retirement fund goal based *just* on this 70 percent to 100 percent rule. If I knew I was going to live to 100, then it would be easier! I would just need to pull out my calculator and multiply my yearly salary in the years leading up to retirement by the number of years between my retirement and age 100, and I would be good to go. Pack it up folks, we have a number! But since there is an unknown element here, we need to take another factor into account. I'll let you guess what that is…

TWO MINUTE WARNING!

Hopefully you guessed what some might call the eighth wonder of the world: compounding! That's right, the magic of compounding interest don't just disappear when you retire. If you saved up a chunk of money to retire on, that money still *works* for you after you retire. You still earn interest on it, and you can find the sweet spot where you are earning interest at a rate that lets you live at a level very close to your pre-retirement one without **a)** having to know how long you will need money, and **b)** without worrying about running out of cheddar! All right, this doesn't sound very sexy, but the way the math works is actually very cool, and it means you can kick back and enjoy yourself without having to constantly monitor your finances. I know you are probably going crazy with excitement to see some equations, but before we talk about how to make interest work for you *after* retirement, there is one more topic to cover. I've been saving the best for last, because it is free money!

THAT THING PEOPLE TALK ABOUT ON THE NEWS

If you pay even a small amount of attention to the political world, especially around presidential election time, you have heard politicians and news anchors talk about Social Security. Social Security is a safety net, funded by payroll taxes, that pays out money to workers after they retire. Remember the brief history earlier in this book about FDIC-insured banks? Well, the Social Security system is another government program that was put in place in the aftermath of the stock market crash of 1929 and the ensuing Great Depression. The powers-that-be realized that in order to protect people financially after they stop working, a program would be necessary.

You can actually see your contributions to Social Security right on your paycheck. Most paychecks have a section displaying "statutory deductions," and this is where you can find how much is taken out of your paychecks for federal income tax, Medicare tax, and Social Security tax. A good way to think about it is as a government-run savings account without any interest. As you work and get paid, the federal government deducts some money from your paychecks and puts it into a giant fund. Then, when you retire, you are paid a certain amount each month out of that giant fund. The amount depends on several variables, including what age you were when you retired and started collecting Social Security, and how much you made over the course of your working life, broken down annually. The US Social Security Administration has a calculator on its website that will let you put in your information so you can see what your monthly benefit will be.

Social Security benefits vary quite a bit depending on when you retire and start collecting. You get the maximum benefit if you wait until you are 70 to retire. If you retire before that, you will receive less and less a month. The system bottoms out at age 62; if you retire at 62, you will get the *least* eligible amount possible from Social Security. Exactly when you retire will probably be one of the biggest factors determining your retirement income. This is for two reasons, the first being these Social Security laws. The second reason is one you are now very familiar with (I hope!): the longer you can wait to tap into your 401(k) or IRA, the more compounding and capital appreciation will increase your retirement fund.

Let's look at a few examples so that you can see what Social Security benefits look like based on several different income levels and retirement ages. It is important to realize that Social Security calculations assume that for the most part, you made the same amount of money each year for your entire career. Hopefully this isn't the case, and you're making more over time. So if anything, these numbers will be *lower* than what you should hope for. But for the sake of completing our look at retirement planning, let's just take the numbers at face value.

Let's take someone who earned lower-middle class income, and brought home $36,000 a year. Janet was a librarian and worked hard for many years. Her job didn't cause a lot of wear and tear, so she decides to make the most of her Social Security benefits and waits until age 70 to retire. She will collect the maximum amount allowed by law for this income level, and as of 2017 will receive $1,882 a month in benefits. Now, if she decides to retire at the normal full retirement age (which is sixty-seven), she will receive $1,518 a month. Quite a bit less! And if she decides she is sick of shelving books and just wants to relax on the beach and retires at sixty-two, she will receive $1,069 a month. As you can see, these amounts are wildly different. In Janet's case, working an extra 8 years means she will receive almost double the amount in Social Security benefits. Now we can begin to see just how much this will affect her overall retirement picture. That extra $800 a month that she is *not* earning if she retires early will need to come from somewhere else: her own retirement plan savings! This means she will have to adjust her expectations when it comes to the performance of her 401(k), and will have to aim for a higher goal.

Let's say Janet was a senior Human Resources officer at a large company, and was making $100,000 a year. If she retires at sixty-two, her Social Security payout will be $1,811 a month as of this writing. If she waits until full retirement, she will bring in $2,670 a month. And if she waits until age 70 and gets the max benefit, she will bring in a whopping $3,311 a month. Again, a huge difference in numbers.

THE TWO-LEGGED STOOL

A two-legged stool won't stand up on its own, but your retirement can. These are the chief contributors (for most of us) to retirement success: Social Security, and the retirement plan that you privately funded—hopefully with some help from your employer, be it through stock options or a company match. Now that we can see the whole retirement picture, we can revisit the idea of goals. Let's stick with the alternate-dimension Janet, the one making $100,000 a year in the years leading up to retirement.

Janet is sixty years old and is starting to think about retirement. She decides that after retiring she wants to live fairly close to the level she has grown accustomed to. She wants to eat the same food, take the same vacations, and get a new iPhone each year. She doesn't want to have to micromanage her finances, but also doesn't want to worry about running short on cash. Having decided on this, she is ready to start formulating a goal. The first thing she does is look at how her expenses will change when she retires.

For starters, once she retires she won't have work-related expenses. She won't need new work clothes, and she won't have to pay for gas to drive to and from work. On top of that, her children are all grown up, and she was able to sell her house, pay off her mortgage, and rent a nice cottage on the beach, where she plans on enjoying her retirement. After considering these changes to her expenses, she decides that she would be able to live up to the standards she expects on **80 percent** of the amount she earned each year before retiring. So, she will need access to $80,000 a year, or $6,666 a month.

Now, Janet was always a good planner, and since she worked in Human Resources she knows all about retirement plans and Social Security (and of course, knows the company's 401(k) advisor pretty well and has gotten excellent advice). As a result, she plans to retire when she is seventy. We know from the previous section that this will give her $3,311 a month from Social Security. Look at that—she is halfway there already! This means she will need her 401(k) to make up the remaining $3,355 a month, or $40,260 a year.

Now compounding comes swooping back in to save the day. For the sake of argument, let's say that Janet's 401(k) will experience a consistent percentage growth, both while she is working and after she retires. Janet just needs to figure out the answer to this question: **how much money does she need in her retirement fund when she retires, such that she can use $40,260 a year but not run out of money because the fund is gaining a percentage of interest each year?**

The minimum amount Janet needs to save in order to retire and meet her criteria is about $1 million (**$1,053,554.32**, to be precise). If she has this amount saved up, then she can freely spend her money in the way she did before retiring and never have to worry about running out of money. Her retirement account will basically be earning enough because of compounding that what she spends each year won't reduce the principal, and she can keep on generating money to replace what she spends.

This is about ten times her yearly salary, and it is what I recommend: **In order to retire securely and live in a way comparable to your lifestyle while working, your retirement fund goal should be eight to ten times your annual salary.** The "salary" part here is referring to the five to ten years leading up to retirement. After all, you don't want to retire and have to live the way you did when you were twenty-five years old, living in the apartment and eating Chick-fil-A three times a week, right? You have worked hard and hopefully seen raises and promotions, and you should feel that you have earned a retirement that reflects that.

BUT I'M NOT OLD YET!

You might think this just doesn't apply to you. You aren't Janet. You aren't sixty years old. If you are reading this book, you might be just starting off your career. You might be in college still. You probably don't have a clue where your career will take you or how much money you are going to make. Even if you understand compounding, 401(k)s, and Social Security, how can you possibly begin to apply this knowledge and formulate a **goal** for retirement at your age? Let's hop into David's time traveling chair and work forwards from the beginning, armed with the knowledge you have gained so far.

The answer to the question of how to meet this *final* goal is to meet many *smaller* goals along the way. Meeting these goals will let you, when the time comes, be on track to hit that target of eight to ten times your final salary. You are already familiar with the very first step, which is signing up for a 401(k) or 403(b) if your employer offers one, or starting an IRA on your own if this option isn't available to you. The next step is to determine how much you should contribute to your retirement plan in order to reach the next goalpost. Here are the goalposts (and these are not set in stone by any means):

- By age thirty-five, you should have saved the equivalent of one year's salary.

- By age forty-five, you should have saved the equivalent of three years' salary.

- By age fifty-five, you should have saved the equivalent of five years' salary.

- By retirement age, you should have saved the equivalent of eight to ten years' salary.

These goalposts assume that you start a retirement fund early in your career, around twenty-five years old. Remember way back towards the beginning of the book in the monthly income breakdown, where I talked about contributing 6 percent of your salary to your retirement plan? No? I can't blame you! You're in luck! We'll show that to you.

This is roughly the amount you should contribute to your plan the first year in order to reach the first goalpost. In the second year, you should bump this amount up to 7 percent. In the third year, you should bump it up again to 8 percent. To reach goalpost #1, you should do this each year until you are contributing 12 percent of your income to your retirement plan by age 32.

Let's say you open your account when you are twenty-five years old, and your starting salary is $32,000 per year. Each year, you get an $800 raise. Your initial contribution to your 401(k) is $500, and your plan will experience an 8 percent annual return over the course of your career (capital appreciation, dividends, and interest). If you apply the above guidelines for contributions to your retirement plan, this is what the path to the first goal looks like:

AGE	SALARY	% CONTRIBUTED	$ CONTRIBUTED	TOTAL VALUE
25	$32,000	6% yearly	$1,920	$2,613.60
26	$32,800	7% yearly	$2,296	$5,302.37
27	$33,600	8% yearly	$2,688	$8,629.60
28	$34,400	9% yearly	$3,096	$12,663.65
29	$35,200	10% yearly	$3,520	$17,478.34
30	$36,000	11% yearly	$3,960	$23,153.41
31	$36,800	12% yearly	$4,416	$29,774.96
32	$37,600	12% yearly	$4,512	$37,029.92

So let's look at what this means. You made an initial contribution of $500, and made $26,408 in other contributions over the course of eight years, meaning your total contributions are $26,908. You have made $10,121.92 thanks in part to compounding, and are well on your way to meeting the first goalpost. Let's look at the last few years:

AGE	SALARY	% CONT.	$ CONT.	TOTAL VALUE
33	$38,400	12% yearly	$4,608	$44,968.95
34	$39,200	12% yearly	$4,704	$53,646.79
35	$40,000	12% yearly	$4,800	$63,122.53

You are really picking up steam and have actually blown the first goalpost out of the water! Congratulations! Your total contributions are $41,020, and you're total return so far is a respectable $22,102.53. That's right, your earnings over the last three years are more than **double** what they were for the first eight years! Now, imagine that your employer changes their 401(k) plan in order to make working for them more attractive, and they start matching 50 percent of contributions up to a certain percentage when you are thirty-three years old. Let's see what that would look like for the last three years:

AGE	SALARY	% CONT.	$ CONT.	$ EMP. CONT.	TOTAL VALUE
33	$38,400	12% yearly	$4,608	$2,304	$47,457.27
34	$39,200	12% yearly	$4,704	$2,352	$58,874.33
35	$40,000	12% yearly	$4,800	$2,400	$71,360.28

Are you starting to feel badass yet? You should! As you can see, meeting smaller goals spaced out through your career is the key to reaching retirement success, and it all starts with small contributions at a young age. Just for the sake of completion, let's see what your retirement fund would look like if it stayed this way. If you never get another raise, and you and your employer just keep contributing to your plan at the same level, by the time you are forty-five you will have $266,709. By the time you are fifty-five, you will have $688,452. And by the time you are sixty-seven and ready to retire with solid Social Security benefits, you will have $1,881,206! This is actually fifty-eight times your first year's salary, by the way. Told you it was magic!

THE HIDDEN CHAPTER: ACHIEVEMENT UNLOCKED!

We have finally made it to the end of our journey—through what many think is a financial wasteland—and discovered that it wasn't really that bad. It's actually pretty simple. Simple, *not* easy. There is a difference! Easy things take no effort; they just get done. Simple things require work, but can become easy once you know the rules. Thanks to the lessons of Investor Jones, Jen, and a few other folks, you now have the tools to make the decisions that will prepare you for most financial steps on the road of life. And it didn't kill you! Far from it...it was inspirational.

> *"Don't worry about it, and you'll be rich..."*

> **—said nobody ever.**

2060

It was a slightly overcast day, but the air was still warm. Jen stood in the airport terminal, looking out at the hypersonic jet that would soon take her skipping out above the atmosphere, from L.A. to Switzerland in under 20 minutes. The tech was new enough on the consumer end that passengers needed to pass through special security stations. After being cleared they were given bright blue armbands to show they were allowed on the futuristic hybrid jets. Between that and the incredibly expensive first-class ticket, and thanks to all those miles and points she earned over the years (thank you, VISA!), Jen was in an exclusive club as she stood waiting to board.

"Jen? Holy shit!"

Jen turned and saw a disheveled, cheerful-looking man ambling up to her. He was wearing basic, shapeless brown pants and a matching shirt. He had a yellow armband on: economy class, traditional Airbus 320.

"Jack! Is that you? What a surprise! It's been so long!"

They hugged it out. It *had* been a while! They had kept up sporadically on social media but hadn't seen each other since shortly after college.

"Nice armband," Jack said, "I checked on the web when buying my tickets. Those things are expensive!"

"Yeah," Jen replied, "but it was for a special occasion, and YOLO. This is my first big trip being officially retired!"

Jack laughed. "I remember thinking retirement was a dirty word back when we were kids. It seemed like something we would never have to worry about. I wish sometimes I could go back in time and knock some sense into my past self and change some things. Where are you headed?"

"Switzerland. The Rolling Stones are having a reunion concert and I have pit passes...I'm excited!"

Jack's eyes opened wide. "Wow, living the good life. I thought you ended up in middle management somewhere? Were you secretly a drug dealer or something?"

"Haha, no. I just worked hard like we all do, but paid attention to my investments and retirement funds. It wasn't really that complicated. I learned some lessons early on and figured out a path to retirement that would let me do just about whatever I wanted when the time came. I used to tell you that you really didn't need to be a genius, Jack. Just know the basics, and stick with it through good and bad. There will be a lot of distractions along the way, that's just plain old life! Hell, it was way more emotional than complicated. Don't let it discourage you."

Jen's wrist began chirping, and she flicked her finger to open up the hologram display on her brand-new implant web device.

"And the newest tech too. Pretty impressive! I still carry my phone around in my pocket." Jack shook his head. He was definitely blown away by Jen's lifestyle. He was still working, and retirement wasn't anything he was looking forward to in the near future. He had Social Security waiting in the wings, but he hadn't paid much attention to other retirement fund options. Not to mention, the financial crisis of 2038 spooked him and he panicked and sold most of his stock funds near the bottom. And all these years later, he was still not fully invested.

"Now boarding GalactaJet Flight 1567 to Zurich, zone alpha," a sexy British voice said over the PA system.

"Well, that's me," Jen said, hugging Jack one last time. "Keep in touch, I have a large vacation planned around Jay-Z and Beyonce's summer tour, but we should meet back up when I get back!"

"Of course," Jack replied. "You know, back in high school, I never would have predicted you would end up this successful. Shows what I know! Great to see you Jen...you really are a badass!"

Jen smiled, flicked down her hologram read out, and started walking towards the loading platform. She was first to board the sleek jet. As she settled into her luxurious seat and accepted a tumbler of 2025 Basil Hayden's scotch, she thought back to what Jack had said.

A badass, huh? She thought. She grinned knowingly from ear to ear.

WHERE DO WE GO FROM HERE

You don't need to see 40 years into the future to plan successfully for the future. You just need to know the basics, and you need to start now. Think about where you want your retirement fund to be in ten years, and contribute enough to reach that goal. Once you get there, think about where you want to be in another ten years. Slowly, day by day and dollar by dollar, you will find yourself marching towards wonderful things. And in the meantime, since you've learned a lot about proper budgeting and saving, you'll be able to work towards buying a house and having an emergency fund for all of life's surprises. Trust me, they will happen. It's a wild world out there. As the old saying goes, "Man plans, and God laughs."

This book isn't designed to give you all the answers to financial success. No matter how long and how diligently we plan, shit happens. But I wanted to give you some new cool concepts and a few simple fundamentals. Just like our badass Jen, having success and building wealth does not require great intelligence, a degree in economics, or familiarity with Wall Street jargon, like alpha and beta. Years ago I was just like you; younger, in the same shoes, starting my first job at a bank, of all places, making a starting salary of $28,500. But I had, just like you have now, the most valuable resource: time...and a desire for more!

DANKEST TOGETHER

A financial badass is cutthroat when she needs to be...and compassionate whenever she can be. It isn't easy out there. There is a good chance you haven't been handed anything and have had to claw your way through the educational and professional system to get where you are. You aren't going to waste time on tools that slow you down (0.15 percent interest? Thanks, but no thanks), and you will drop a brand like it's a flaming Note 7 (too soon?).

As fast-paced and tough as the world of DIY-finances can be, you also have amazing opportunities to help one another. Kickstarter, Venmo, and charity apps like Feedie make spreading the wealth to friends and strangers easier than ever before.

Badassery thrives on individual effort, but levels up when it has company. Technology has brought us together, and if you can't do something, chances are you have a friend who can.

So give back, to friends and charities...you never know when it might pay off. And you never know what impact your giving might have!

BONUS SECTION: GIVE IT AWAY!

(THE MOST IMPORTANT ONE!)

Pathos – *a feeling of intense enthusiasm toward or a compelling desire for someone or something*

There is actually one other thing you can do with your money, besides spending it, saving it, or investing it—giving it away. I know, you are probably thinking, *WTF? I worked so hard for this money and gave up so much to save it and invest it properly. It has grown, after all that work... why would I give it away?*

Because giving it away is what badasses *do.* They give back to someone who needs it more than they do, they give to groups or causes that are close to them, that speak to them, that they are passionate about helping or seeing succeed. There are over 1.5 million non-profits in the United States. Trust me, whichever cause you find passion about today, or later in life, chances are there is a non-profit or charity that focuses on exactly that cause.

And now, there's one more.

Project 10.10 was started well before this book went to print. The mission is simple—to educate and enlighten young people to realize their dreams, unlock their potential, and take charge of their financial futures. All proceeds of Project 10.10 will be given to organizations that make this happen.

How will Project 10.10 raise money, you might ask? Well, you have already helped. Part of the proceeds of the sales of what you just read (this book!) will be given to Project 10.10. This is a brand-new charity, starting with nothing. But we *will* grow it and we *will* make a difference; after all, we have already been there, done that, and we know how this works!

I know it might be hard to wrap your head around the notion that giving your money away can be so gratifying and feel so good. But trust me, when in your life you find a cause (and yes, you can have more than one) that moves you and that you care about, giving to that cause will feel better than spending!

One last thing…if you are wondering how I came up with the name Project 10.10, it was pretty simple. Back on the Friday I gave that excellent meeting, from the story in the intro…the date was October 10th, 2014.

NO QUARTER!

Our first mission was to learn something about saving. Moral of the story there: it might be hard while you are doing it, but truth be told, it becomes simple once you put your mind to it. Whether you need a budget or not (who are we kidding, of course you need one!), the resources are out there to guide you. Next, we learned about smarter ways to spend your money—the power of utilizing credit, and avoiding the pitfalls of easy credit and taking on too much debt.

After that, you aced the sections that deal with my true passion—investing. I consider myself lucky that investing caught my attention as early as it did. When I was in high school the bug got me, and I have been obsessed with it ever since. I suppose I was also lucky that one of my earliest and strongest interests was one that could make money! One of my main goals in writing this book was to teach you the basics of investing in capital markets by participating in your company-sponsored retirement plan.

Finally, you learned that it's so much fun making money! A bookie once said, "Money won is so much sweeter than money earned." (Of course he did!) Well, I'm here to tell you—money made when you invest is the sweetest of all. When you buy in and own a piece of company that is thriving, disrupting their industry, kicking ass and taking names, and then the stock goes up, up, and away—that's f-ing powerful! Being on the right side of financial history, even if just for a few months—making that right choice and putting your money where your mouth is—when it pays off, not much is as satisfying as that!

But more than anything—if you take just one lesson from this project, let it be the story of our two heroes, Jack and Jen. The few simple things that Jen did at certain key moments in her life made all the difference. She made the right moves early and consistently. Most importantly, remember that she wasn't the smartest or the cleverest in school, she certainly wasn't a financial whiz, and she didn't have to attend an Ivy League school to end up where she did. Hell, she didn't even major in business!

What she did was center on a few key points that should be the major takeaways:

1. Save early, have a budget, and have goals.
2. Spend wisely, in a way that supports your goals.
3. Invest early.
4. Max out your contributions.
5. Do not get spooked by the ups and downs, and stay in the market!

Take risks early in life with stocks. The real risk isn't losing money…it's not earning the highest possible rate of return on your money. The point is you don't have to master this stuff to be a successful badass. You don't have to read the *Wall Street Journal* every day just to break even. Time is on your side, so stay in and win. Just *own it!* I have said that sort of thing repeatedly, so I'll go for it one last time. These decisions, made early on, *can* and *do* lead to wealth down the road. Remember, wealth is freedom. And you are the master.

Financial freedom, whether you want to call it "substantial retirement savings" or "screw you" money—it all means the same thing. You have the power to take control of your finances, and by extension, your life. Don't take any prisoners. Stick to your principles and become dangerous. Having enough money saved up, knowing that you can do whatever you want without having to worry about what might happen next—that is what Jen did. That is what badasses *do*.

ACKNOWLEDGMENTS

To my mom and dad. Thank you for your incredible support, love, and inspiration. You had one simple dream when you arrived in this country: for your children to live a better life. You've given me everything.

To my wonderful business partners, who are much more than just friends and mentors. Bob and Mike, you guys rock! Land, you make us better every day. I'm lucky to be on your team.

To the entire gang at Mascot Books: Naren, Chris, Danny, Kristin, and everyone else. Thank you for believing in my story and the vision I had for this book as much as I did.

Last but not least, to everyone on Team FinBadass: my brother, Billy, John, Michelle, Kristen, Barbara, Jon, Greg, Marnie, Jacqueline, and countless others. Thank you not only for your support, patience, and feedback, but more so for your eternal friendship and loyalty. You are the real badasses.

EXTRA READING

**Psych Yourself Rich: Get the Mindset and Discipline
You Need to Build Your Financial Life**
by Farnoosh Torabi

I Will Teach You To Be Rich
by Ramit Sethi

**How to Retire with Enough Money:
And How to Know What Enough Is**
by Teresa Ghilarducci

The Money Book for the Young, Fabulous & Broke
by Suze Orman

MONEY: Master the Game: 7 Simple Steps to Financial Freedom
by Tony Robbins

**The Wealthy Barber: Everyone's Commonsense Guide
to Becoming Financially Independent**
by David Chilton

Rich Dad Poor Dad
by Robert T. Kiyosaki

The Bogleheads' Guide to Investing
by Taylor Larimore, Mel Lindauer, and Michael LeBoeuf

https://www2.ed.gov/fund/grants-apply.html?src=ft
https://www.creditkarma.com/
https://www.annualcreditreport.com/

Now, some of these books were written a while ago, like *Rich Dad Poor Dad*. That doesn't mean that they are outdated, though. Even the older books on this list are full of great advice and important principles, many of which you were introduced to in this book. Things like taking the long-term approach, making savings a priority, and not thinking you can predict the market...this is good advice no matter what.

GLOSSARY

401(k) – a retirement plan that grows thanks to compounding, dividends, and capital appreciation and is managed by an employer, fueled by pre-tax dollars.

403(b) – like a 401(k), but usually offered by schools and non-profits.

Bonds – stable investments that grow at a steady rate over a certain period of time.

Brokerage – a business that arranges purchases of shares.

Capital – wealth in the form of money or assets of a company or individual.

Capital Appreciation – the combination of compounding and asset value growth of an investment.

Certificates of Deposit – a bank account that grows over a fixed amount of time, like a bond.

Checking Account – a bank account that doesn't earn interest; used primarily for purchases.

Compounding – interest growth over time, built on previous interest earnings.

Credit Union – a type of bank owned by account holders.

Dividends – periodic payouts from companies to shareholders.

Index – a performative list of companies used to track market health.

Index Fund – a mutual fund that is mapped to a particular stock market index, like the S&P 500.

Inflation – a general increase in prices and fall in the purchasing value of money.

Interest – growth of a fund based on established rates.

IRA – a retirement plan that is managed by the individual holding the plan, fueled by after-tax dollars.

Money Market Account – a type of bank account characterized by high interest and limited withdrawal ability.

Mutual Funds – funds invested in by groups of people, made up of different types of investments, with a single fund manager.

Pension – a long-term retirement plan offered by a company that periodically pays out based on salary and time worked.

Roth IRA – an IRA that features tax-free withdrawals.

Savings Account – a bank account that earns interest; used for saving money for long-term purchases.

SEP IRA – an IRA offered by smaller companies, with tax deductible contributions.

Shares – certificates of ownership of a portion of a company's capital.

Social Security – a US government program that pays out monthly amounts after retirement based on retirement age and past earnings.

Stock – capital raised by a company through the issue and subscription of shares.

INDEX

NOTES

NOTES